Saviour of the Nation

Saviour
of the Nation

An epic poem of
Winston Churchill's finest hour

BRIAN HODGKINSON

SHEPHEARD-WALWYN (PUBLISHERS) LTD

First published in 2015 by
Shepheard-Walwyn (Publishers) Ltd
107 Parkway House, Sheen Lane,
London SW14 8LS
www.shepheard-walwyn.co.uk

British Library Cataloguing in Publication Data
A catalogue record of this book
is available from the British Library

ISBN: 978-0-85683-506-3

Typeset by Alacrity, Chesterfield, Sandford, Somerset
Printed and bound in the United Kingdom
by imprint*digital*.com

Contents

Preface

Winston Churchill was the greatest Englishman of the twentieth century, and perhaps the greatest of all time.* His life was immensely rich and varied, for he excelled in the fields of politics, war, statesmanship and literature. Yet his crowning achievement was, without question, his leadership of Britain and the British Empire and Commonwealth during the Second World War. Even within that, his supreme qualities of courage, resolution and inspiring oratory were concentrated in the period from the outbreak of war in 1939 until the entry of the USA into the war in December 1941. Hence any literary work that tries to capture the essence of the man needs to focus likewise on this relatively short period when Britain fought for its survival against Nazi Germany. Especially is this so when the literary form is narrative poetry, where facts and historical detail are secondary to emotional intensity. As far as possible, I have adhered to recorded history within the limitations of the principal sources used and my own recollection of wider reading over many years. However, the selection of facts has been influenced by the overall demand for dramatic impact.

In particular the direct speeches made by Churchill in the poem are no more than paraphrases with a few words taken from what he actually said. This is necessitated by the need to avoid actual quotation, but especially by the demands of conciseness and metre. Personally I do not believe that Churchill himself would have objected to any attempt, however inadequate, to portray him as an epic hero.

* In 2002 he was named as the greatest Briton of all time in a nation-wide poll conducted by the BBC, attracting more than a million votes.

1 The Menace of Nazi Germany
Winter 1933

Throughout the night the drum of marching feet
And flickering light from torches held aloft
Engrossed the streets of many German towns;
Whilst in Berlin the aged President
Saluted from his balcony the troops
Of *Sturmabteilung*, *Stahlhelm* and S.S.,
Whose banners rose in white and red and black.
And watching, too, with burning eyes of zeal,
Stood Adolf Hitler, now the Chancellor.

In that great land of prehistoric myth,
Of mighty rivers, darkest forest, lakes,
Of Alpine peaks that cast long shades of night
And bar the way to Bacchus' revelries,
A deep resentment warped the souls of men.
The lust of Mars, the pride of nationhood,
Abruptly had been shamed. For many years,
The warlike Germans could not carry arms.
Their massive guns, steel-plated battleships,
And marching ranks of millions, bold and loyal,
Obedient to fatherland and king,
Had vanished at the word of armistice.

Thus mortal wounds, inflicted by defeat
And violent insurrection, doomed the State
Which followed on the Versailles settlement.
It was an interregnum for all those
Who smouldered with desire to be avenged.
Some, like Stresemann, tried to quench the fire,
But few would stand by Weimar and the law.
Bruning and Streicher struggled to enforce

Their vain attempts at sweeping compromise,
Till Papen came, a former Chancellor,
To woo the careworn President with hope
That, once in office, Hitler would be bound
By cabinet colleagues, like the Nationalists.
"We'll box him in!" brave Hugenberg had said,
And few, beyond the Nazis, could believe
That Corporal Hitler, but a demagogue,
Would govern long unruly Germany.
Yet soon he showed his innate ruthlessness.
The violence of his language won support
From all those Germans keen to see destroyed
The Treaty of Versailles, and those who feared
That Jews and Marxists threatened Germany.
He called for new elections, claiming these
Would but confirm his own supremacy.

Before the votes were cast the Reichstag fire
Had burnt to ashes hopes of real reform.
The stormtroop legions cast aside restraint.
When Goring sanctioned police atrocities,
The Communists were murdered, or were held
Without due trial, regardless of the law.
A presidential edict had destroyed
All guarantees of personal liberty;
The new Republic, handicapped from birth
By enemies of freedom – *Freikorps* bands
And revolutionaries of left and right –
Was strangled by the senile Hindenburg.

At Potsdam, where the Prussian kings had sat,
Old memories of the *Kaiserreich* were stirred
When Hitler bowed before the head of State,
And wreaths were laid on tombs of monarchy.
But two days later all pretence was gone.
The Reichstag met in Berlin's Opera House
To grant to Hitler unrestricted power.

Before the doors the *Sturmabteilung* stood,
Jackbooted brownshirts, eyeing delegates.
Inside, their comrades ringed the chamber walls.
Despite such terror, Otto Wells spoke out,
A final voice of liberal Germany,
Against the certain passage of the Bill
That gave to Hitler overwhelming powers.
Wells could not win. Too many absentees,
Deprived of rights, were held in custody.
This overture to German tragedy
Now set the scene for crude dictatorship.
The State would be the instrument of men
Obsessed by hate and racial fantasies.
The road to war was opened to the tread
Of German armies soon revitalised.

To Adolf Hitler war had been a dream,
Which offered him a kind of comradeship
In risk and violence, bravery and will.
When, as a youth, he'd seen so many Jews
Within his Austrian homeland, when he'd read
Hypotheses of racial purity,
And heard condemned the role of German Jews
In business, banking, law and medicine,
His mind was warped by unremitting rage:
Marxism was the Jew's conspiracy,
Now thriving in that Slavic hinterland
Where Germany demanded *Lebensraum*.
The Nordic race must claim its destiny
And rid itself of all but German stock.
By war a race survives, by right of strength.
Destroy the rule of parties and of laws
That do not bear the German people's will.
Ein Reich, ein Volk, ein Führer; thus it was.

2 The Prophet Unheeded
Summer 1932

Winston Churchill, of the famous line
Descended from the Duke of Marlborough,
Had stayed in Munich, just before the rise
Of Adolf Hitler to dictatorship.
In that same city, which not long before,
Had seen the police shoot down a Nazi band,
Who'd planned to seize the reins of government,
A meeting was arranged. For Churchill then
Had little knowledge of this violent man,
Who was to be his chief protagonist.
Against Herr Hitler, at this time, he said,
He had no national prejudice, nor knew
What views he held, what type of man he was;
He had the right to be a patriot,
To stand up for his country in defeat.
But Hitler learned that Churchill had enquired
About the Jews. Why did he hate them so?
No more advances came from either side.
The arch-opponents of the future war
Would never see each other face to face.

Though he had held high offices of State,
Now Winston Churchill sat in Parliament
Below the aisle, a lonely figure, shunned,
A critic of his party's policies.
Rotund and short, and stooping from a blow
Received in playing polo in his youth,
He yet retained a charismatic power.
His smooth and pinkish face, with glaucous eyes,
Set 'neath a lofty brow and balding head,
Could be expressive when he was aroused.

But often now he looked more in repose,
In brooding thought on matters secretive,
As one – for those who knew him – like a fire,
Damped down, but waiting, incubated, dulled,
Yet burning still with concentrated heat.

Most doubted now his judgment, since that time
When, in the former war, he'd pressed the case
For Allied action in the Dardanelles.
How much he'd suffered from that cruel debacle,
Fought out on shores of far Gallipoli!
Without full power, yet ardent to pursue
A plan to end the slaughter in the west,
He'd watched its failure, grieved at its mistakes,
And mourned for those who'd perished there in vain.

He listened now to lesser men's debates.
Prime Minister MacDonald was not loth
To press upon the European powers
The need to hasten their disarmament.
Widespread opinion favoured such a course.
Had not the war been caused by armaments?
The losers had been stripped of all their power,
But, of the victors, France especially,
Retained its forces in preponderance.
Should not the French and others acquiesce
By cutting down their arms to parity?
The British government did not make a stand
Against this plea from vanquished enemies.
Indeed they showed displeasure at the French
For clinging to their own security.
For Britain had not witnessed German troops
Trample the growing corn of native land,
And seen their ancient villages subdued
By field-grey soldiers, alien in tongue.
Yet France would keep her army, though some knew,
Like Charles de Gaulle, it was not competent.

Amidst these cries of fear and sentiment,
One voice in England spoke of principles:
'Whilst grievances of vanquished States remain,
It is not safe for victors to disarm.'
Churchill did not ignore the Germans' case
For some amendment of the harshest terms
Imposed by post-war treaty at Versailles:
Their loss of land, their weakness in defence
In view of Russia's greater armaments,
Their economic burdens, and the guilt
Which they regarded as unjustly borne.
And yet to see them arming for revenge
Was to invite a new catastrophe.

It was not long ago that he himself
Had argued for the British to reduce
Expenditure on arms. As Chancellor,
He'd forced the British Admiralty to cut
Its spending on new cruisers; then refused
To finance a new base at Singapore.
And later he'd advised the Cabinet
To keep the rule that war was not foreseen
For ten years in the future. Now he knew
How circumstances differed; how once more
The world was threatened with the bane of war.

So Churchill braved the judgment of his peers;
'Thank God', he cried, 'that France has not disarmed.'
Though even he did not expect the war
That Germans, like von Seekt, had now conceived:
A war of movement, blitzkrieg, planes and tanks.
Instead he feared the flames in city streets,
The hail of bombs on helpless citizens.
For he well knew the face of war had changed.
As First Lord of the Admiralty, he'd known
How every ship was armed; how they must match
The German Dreadnoughts and the submarines

Within the North Sea and the ocean deeps.
One admiral then, he'd said, could lose the war;
In one engagement all could be at risk.
But aircraft had transformed the art of war.
Britain, especially, was most vulnerable,
With massive cities, ports and industries
And London within minutes of the coast.
He was appalled to hear the government say
That no new squadrons were to be equipped;
That Britain's air force was the fifth air power.
What scorn he poured on Baldwin's later claim
That he'd not called for due rearmament,
Because he'd feared to lose too many votes!

Within the Civil Service some men felt
The need to give support to Churchill's views,
For they, like him, envisaged Britain's plight
If she was soon outpaced in armaments.
They secretly informed him of the news
About the German programme, whilst he too
Obtained from agents on the continent
Material to further his critique
Of Baldwin and his government's policy.

3 Office Denied
Summer 1934

From Germany a fearsome signal came
Of what dire evil gathered there unchecked.
The leader of the *Sturmabteilung*, Roehm,
Was not content with Hitler's policies,
Especially for the army, which Roehm saw
As still the Prussian hierarchy's preserve,
A bastion of social privilege
Denied to those who'd fought for Nazi power
With rallies, marches, violence in the streets.
Stormtroopers, or the *Wehrmacht*? Which would hold
The sword of execution in the State?

Though Hitler was reluctant to condemn
A comrade from the Munich barricades,
He did not dare offend the army's pride.
Upon the *Wehrmacht* all his hopes were built
Of future war, of German dominance.
With its connivance, Roehm was soon destroyed –
S.S. gunmen shot him down unarmed –
With others who might threaten the regime.
To justify the murders, Hitler claimed
That fateful hour had made him arbiter,
Responsible for German destiny
And thus empowered to disregard the law.
When Churchill heard of this dark episode,
It but confirmed his view of Nazidom.

Yet British leaders still retained some trust
That Hitler's word could be relied upon.
They signed a naval treaty, which defined
A limit to the German *Kriegsmarine*.

Henceforth it could not build beyond a third
Of British strength, except in submarines.
Churchill condemned it. Did it not ignore
The limitations still applicable?
Moreover, Churchill knew that not for years
Could Germany construct beyond this norm.
How could the British claim still to respect
Collective action 'gainst the German threat,
When now they came to terms bilateral?
The world could see', he said, 'they had connived
At Germany's undue rearmament.'

The hope of peace was struck another blow
By Mussolini's greed in Africa.
To claim revenge for Adowa's defeat
And build an Italian empire in the south,
The Fascist leader wilfully attacked
The ancient State of Ethiopia.
It was not long since Churchill had approved
Of Mussolini as a lawgiver;
But now the *Duce* clearly had transgressed
The common rules of international law.

A hard dilemma faced the Western powers.
Though Italy had previously opposed
All Nazi plans to coerce Austria,
If France and Britain did not acquiesce
In Italy's unwarranted attack,
The Fascist State might turn to Germany.
Churchill realised this, yet he advised
That international law was paramount.
The British followed League of Nations' plans
For economic sanctions, but these proved
Much weakened by omission of the oil
That drove the wheels of Mussolini's force.

Yet Churchill knew that greater danger lay
In what was happening inside Germany.

For Adolf Hitler, now the Head of State,
Whom every German soldier swore to serve –
Since Hindenburg had died – against advice
Of cautious generals, sent a *Wehrmacht* force
Across the Rhine to occupy the zone
Devoid of troops since Germany's defeat.
This was a flagrant challenge to those powers
Who'd signed two treaties with the Weimar State
That guaranteed the western *status quo*.
It was a gamble. Hitler knew his troops
Could not withstand a major French assault.
But he discerned infirmity of will,
And deep divisions, doubt, and dread of war,
Besetting now the populace of France.

No leader, like the tiger Clemenceau,
Would bend the springs of French resilience.
To Britain Monsieur Flandin looked for help,
Yet Baldwin would do nothing but protest.
The Germans, it was said, had only moved
Into their own back-garden. Hitler drew
Some sure conclusions from his enterprise:
The Western allies would not make a stand;
Their leaders were both timid and corrupt,
Their people feeble, crippled by the fear
Of Armageddon. Whilst in Germany,
They cheered the Austrian corporal's bold success.

Meanwhile, Churchill was contemptuous
Of Baldwin's prevarication and delay:
'They cannot make their minds up. They go on,
Decided in indecision, and resolved
On being always most irresolute.
They're firm for drift, and impotent in power!'

At this key juncture some had pressed the right
Of Churchill to return to government,

And he himself still coveted the chance
Of moving in the corridors of power.
How much he yearned for office once again:
To speak his mind with due authority,
No longer but to cajole and persuade
These purblind men, who ruled in ignorance.
But Baldwin's weakness would not let him turn
To one who stood for firmness. He foresaw
Fierce arguments within the Cabinet room,
Across the table Winston's angry face,
The pointed finger, blunt acerbic phrase,
The facts divulged by sympathetic friends,
The unrelenting will, the wish to act.

Only a few M.P.s and journalists
Supported Churchill's claim. So once again,
The aging statesman laid ambition down,
And sought for solace at his Chartwell home –
Upon a tree-crowned hill in northern Kent –
Where he took up his pen, and set his mind
On follies of more distant history.
He nursed his grievance, England's tragedy.
But, in the country, pressure groups were formed,
Who saw the need for forthright leadership.

Though journalism earned him high rewards,
Expensive social life and personal tastes
Incurred large bills, besides the heavy cost
Of life at Chartwell, where the house employed
A range of servants, from a governess
To bailiff, groom and several gardeners.
Clementine, his wife, was always loyal.
His marriage was secure; but troubles came
From wayward children. Headstrong Randolph,
Brave, indeed, but rash, was entertaining hopes
Of having a political career,
Against his father's contrary advice.

'An animal love connects us' Churchill said,
'But, when we meet, we have a bloody row'.
One daughter recently had been divorced.
Another, Sarah, was about to wed
An entertainer Churchill did not like,
Not least because he was a Viennese,
Twice married and much older than his bride.
Mary, the youngest child, was still at school.
And so, despite some disappointed hopes,
Churchill loved his children, and declined
To let their faults distract him from his task.
And later, in the war, they all would play
An active part, of which he would be proud.

In Parliament he was still moved to speak:
'Now, like the Great War's line of Hindenburg,
Across the western front a fortress wall
Would soon be built of bunkers, mines and guns.
Then German arms could turn upon the Slavs.'
He made a sweeping gesture with his hands,
As though he saw the Germans surging through
The undefended borders to the east.
'No more could Poland, nor the French *entente*
Of Yugoslavs, Roumanians and Czechs,
Expect assistance from the western States.
Even Russia was more vulnerable.
Who now could stop the *Anschluss*? Who could know
The sequel to the *Führer*'s overture?'

But Churchill's hopes of office were destroyed.
Edward of England, recently enthroned,
Became enamoured of a divorcee,
The American Mrs Simpson, disinclined
To rest content as mistress of a king.
Supported by the Church and by *The Times*,
Baldwin opposed the marriage. Even so,
Against this powerful triad, Churchill spoke

Of Edward's right to personal happiness.
Established interests were too strong for him.
King Edward chose his wife and not the crown.
His brother George succeeded in his place,
And Churchill's judgment was again denounced
As lacking wisdom, and impetuous.

Whatever chance remained for his return
Was cast away by loyalty to a king.
None knew, not even he, what hand of fate,
Protected him by failure. None would say
That he had held high office in the land
When policy had erred, when war was caused
By gross mistakes and lack of readiness.

4 Appeasement
Spring 1937

Upon the stage of British politics
Another actor rose to eminence.
The time had come for Baldwin to withdraw.
His powers were waning; he was not the man
To meet the challenge posed by Hitler's threats.
Succeeding him came Neville Chamberlain,
A man of conscience, self-assured, austere,
Who brought to government much efficiency
Acquired by years in peacetime offices.
He sought to understand the claims of those
Who threatened to disrupt the world's affairs:
If he could meet dictators face to face,
Discuss at length their problems, then assess
What compromise might meet their due demands,
Then none would have recourse to violent means.
Such was his view – negotiate, appease.
The path he trod, convinced of rectitude,
Was far too strait for men of Churchill's ilk.

When Chamberlain soon planned to recognise
Italian claims on Ethiopia,
Eden resigned as Foreign Minister.
Henceforth he joined with that tiny band
Who stood opposed to Chamberlain's designs,
And recognised increasingly the need
For Churchill's hand on Britain's helm of State.
The sacrifice of office Eden made
Awoke in Churchill feelings of respect,
And yet he also felt a dark despair
At this new step towards the brink of war.

Hitler was not chastened by the thought
That Chamberlain would meet his just demands.
Once more he'd break the treaty, threatening now
The *Anschluss* with his native Austria.
Courageously the Chancellor Schuschnigg tried
To show by plebiscite his country's will,
But Hitler's fury swept away such hopes.
Where music once had charmed the Viennese,
In Summer parks and vacant palaces,
There echoed now the clattering of tanks,
With harsh commands and footsteps of the Reich.

Just at the time when German soldiers marched
To implement the *Anschluss*, there occurred
A luncheon party at 10 Downing Street.
The guest of honour was von Ribbentrop,
Departing as the Reich's ambassador,
To be, instead, its Foreign Minister.
Churchill, too, was present, and observed
A note was passed to Neville Chamberlain,
Who then seemed worried and pre-occupied.
Deliberately the Ribbentrops stayed late,
As though to hamper Chamberlain's desire
To take some action over Austria.
When Churchill rose to leave, and said he hoped
That Anglo-German friendship would endure,
The wife of the ambassador was curt;
'Make sure you do not spoil it!' she replied.

The British government only could protest;
But Churchill spoke in quite another vein,
When, on the morrow, he addressed the House:
'Again a solemn treaty is ignored,
To build, so it is claimed, a greater State;
Yet it transfers the Ostreich's minerals,
And access to the Danube waterway.
Now south-east Europe lies at Hitler's feet,

And Czechs and Slovaks henceforth are besieged.
How can appeasement check the *Führer*'s will?'

Already *Wehrmacht* generals had prepared
A detailed plan to seize Bohemia.
The pretext was the Czech Sudetenland,
Where Germans claimed they were deprived of rights.
A Nazi party there became the tool
For Hitler's pressure on the Czech regime.
Their leader, Henlein, would not compromise.
At Hitler's bidding all he would accept
Was full succession to the German Reich.

In Berlin's *Sportspalast* the *Führer* spoke,
Calling the German people to their fate:
To fight for *Lebensraum*, for blood and race.
His petty figure, with a small moustache
And puffy features, grey hypnotic eyes,
Black thinning hair that fell across his brow,
Was magnified by words of monstrous power,
Harsh consonants and long emphatic vowels
That rose within him, surging from his throat
With growing volume as the speech progressed.
His grimaces and deft, expressive hands
Conveyed swift moods of satire, or of hate,
And angry exultation. Those who heard
Were moved from dull respect, or apathy,
To yearn for action, violence and revenge.

Upon their mountain lines the Czechs stood firm,
Expecting help from France. Across the world,
The news predicted European war.
At Scapa Flow the naval squadrons watched
For submarines and pocket battleships.
In London air defences were alert.
Trenches were dug amidst the Autumn leaves;
Near public buildings sentries stood on guard.

At main line stations children waved goodbye,
En route to farms and distant cottages.
This was the dress rehearsal for a war
No more confined to fields of Picardy.

No treaty bound the British to the Czechs,
And Chamberlain was eager to redress
Those grievances he thought were genuine.
Alone he flew to Nazi Germany
To wrangle with the *Führer* face to face.
Nothing could be agreed. A last appeal
Was made to Hitler for a conference.
At Munich airport Chamberlain was hailed
By SS guards of honour. There they met,
The Premiers of Britain and of France,
The *Duce* and the *Führer* of the Reich,
To sign away the freedom of the Czechs.
'This is my final claim', the *Führer* said,
'On territory of European States.'
To London Neville Chamberlain returned,
Proclaiming, as Disraeli once had done,
That peace with honour came from Germany.

In Parliament the great majority
Acclaimed with cheers the Premier's success,
And, in the country, who did not rejoice
That war had been averted? Who would dare
To speak against what Chamberlain had done
And brave the odium of decent men,
Who did not see his terrible mistake
In thinking he could trust the *Führer's* word.

So, in the House, when Churchill rose to say
That we'd sustained a terrible defeat,
A total and unmitigated loss,
A storm of protest interrupted him.
But he continued, standing there unmoved,

Peering above his glasses at these men
Whose views he scorned. 'Why have we failed to pledge
The safety of the brave and stubborn Czechs?
Now all is over. Silent and bereft,
The Czech Republic falls in the abyss;
Her people ruined, industry curtailed,
And worst of all, the line of forts is lost –
What is to stop the German conqueror?
This is the grievous consequence of years
Of futile good intentions and neglect
Of British power, especially in the air.
We stand devoid of strength, now, in this hour.
In eastern Europe there is little choice.
Each power will seek the best terms it can get.
The Danube valley, with its corn and oil,
Is open to the Germans. From Berlin
Will radiate a new economy.
Relieved of all anxiety in the east,
The Nazi rulers have a freer choice.
Next year their army will exceed the French.
We have but added four battalions here,
Whilst Germany has gained in hundreds more.
We have not just abandoned one small State,
A long way off, as once our Premier said,
And of which we know nothing. Not at all!
We have to think of what the Nazis are.
Of German people we make no complaint;
Our hearts go out to them. They have no power.
But, with their Nazi leaders, nothing more
Than diplomatic contacts should be made.
Our democratic life and Nazi rule
Can have no friendship. Are we to depend
Upon their will; to meet with their demands?'

At this point Churchill paused. He looked most grim,
And rubbed his hands, quite slowly, on his coat,
The fingers all extended, whilst he thought,

And then, as though selecting every phrase,
He spoke again, yet more deliberately.

'What measures can we take in our defence?
Our island's independence has been lost
By weakness in the air. We must regain it.
All our efforts must seek this one end:
Creation of an air force strong enough
To vanquish any that may reach our shores.
I do not grudge our people – brave and loyal,
Who never flinched last week beneath the strain –
I do not grudge them their relief and joy
At learning that they would not have to face
The worst ordeal at this, the present, time.
But they should know the truth; that we sustained,
Without a war, defeat. That we have passed
A milestone in our history, and have seen
The whole of Europe terribly deranged.
Do not suppose that this is now the end.
This is the foretaste of a bitter cup,
Which will be proffered to us year by year.'

Though in the country many came to feel
That Churchill's view was right – that none could trust
The word of Adolf Hitler – only few,
Amongst the politicians, lent support:
Eden, Bracken, Boothby, Nicolson,
And now Duff Cooper, who alone resigned
In protest at the Munich settlement.

Yet soon new evidence of Nazi crime
Was shown to the world. A Jewish youth,
Outraged by how his parents were expelled
From where they lived at home in Germany,
Shot dead a German diplomat in France.
The Nazis seized upon this incident.
Throughout the Reich the stormtroops ran amok.

Jews were tormented, beaten up or killed,
Or forced to do humiliating tasks,
Like scrubbing paving stones in city streets.
Their synagogues were burnt, their houses wrecked,
Their property was stolen or destroyed.
'I can remember', Clement Attlee said,
'How once when Churchill told me of the Jews,
That, as he spoke, the tears poured down his cheeks.'
Now on the bright Kurfurstendamm there lay,
Where rich Berliners nonchalantly strolled,
The broken glass of Jewish window fronts.

Already Hitler's generals had been told
To plan an armed assault upon the Czechs.
Internal chaos would be his excuse,
For in Slovakia ambition grew
For independence from the rule of Prague.
Whilst Nazi agents fostered this intent,
The *Führer* met the Slovak Premier.
The Czech Republic's aging President
Was forced to call for Germany's support.
Without a shot, the *Wehrmacht* entered Prague.
Steel helmets ringed the statue of Jan Hus,
First martyr for his people's liberty;
And high above Hradcany castle flew
The swastika of red and white and black.
Czechs had not shouted, like Sudeten Deutsch,
Like Rhinelanders and many Austrians,
For German rulers, for the *Herrenvolk*.
This was invasion of a foreign State.

How many dreams were shattered by this news!
Appeasement was dismissed, and Chamberlain,
Who did not like to find he'd been deceived,
Now pledged support for Poland; though he knew
That only Russians could defend the Poles –
And they would not be welcomed. Many saw

That Churchill's warnings now were justified;
And in the press, in homes and clubs and bars,
Where people spoke reluctantly of war,
Persistent murmurs grew for his return.

On Poland now the *Führer*'s venom turned.
The British government, bound to its support,
Could not ignore the part that Russia played.
Yet Chamberlain was cautious. Who could trust
A nation in the hands of Bolsheviks?
To some in Britain, Hitler was the shield
Against the Marxist threat to western powers,
Just as – they argued – Franco had preserved
The Spanish nation from the Soviets.
And so a minor diplomat was sent
To come to terms with Stalin, who himself
Had little cause to welcome such a pact.
Had Britain helped the Czechs? What would they do
To come to the assistance of the Poles?

Such doubts and hesitations bred the chance
For Hitler to astound the world again.
For years he had abused the Soviets
As Communists and agents of the Jews,
But now he looked to short-term strategies
To isolate his foes. The time was ripe
To deal with Poland; so on either side
The seeds of crude hypocrisy were sown.
Negotiations secretly began,
Even whilst the British envoy sat
In futile talks with Stalin's acolytes.

Beyond midsummer England's mood had changed.
In Parliament and populace alike
The belief arose that war was imminent.
The pledge to Poland would not be disowned.
Meanwhile Churchill visited the French,

Questioned their generals, cast a careful eye
On troops and weapons, maps and battle plans.
He noted how the Rhine was well secured,
But how the Ardennes forest offered scope
For armoured groups to hide from air assault.
The French, he saw, no longer countenanced
A vehement attack – no more *la gloire* –
But favoured now invincible defence,
Especially on the line of Maginot.
Yet even he did not appreciate
How vulnerable this was. It will not break,
Without the enemy suffering heavy loss,
And then, meanwhile, the battle could be won,
Was his conclusion, much as others thought.

On his return, the shocking news was heard
Of Ribbentrop's success. A pact was signed
Between the two opposed dictatorships.
Stalin obtained a *cordon sanitaire*
Along the Baltic shores, and Hitler won
Unhindered power to terrorise the Poles.
Once more partition would be Poland's fate.
The chill of Autumn touched all English hearts.
War now was certain. Yet, released from doubt,
The people were at once more resolute.

Britain confirmed the Polish guarantee,
And put her air defences on alert.
Reservists were called up, and on the sea
The navy watched, once more, for submarines.
Where now were allies strong enough to check
The menace of a re-armed Germany?
Towards the great republic in the west
The hopes of Churchill turned. Was he himself
Not half American? His broadcast speech
Appealed to values shared: a common tongue,
The love of freedom, and a firm belief

In what the founding fathers had decreed –
That no one is above the rule of law –
As one man was in Nazi Germany.
Already, in his mind, he had conceived
The vision of a western partnership,
A grand alliance, whose abundant wealth
Would render it, in time, invincible.

Meanwhile Hitler raged against the Poles,
And, on a pretext, German armies struck.
A battleship bombarded Danzig's port.
From London Neville Chamberlain still sent
A last despairing plea to save the peace.
The German Chancellor did not reply.
In Parliament the nation's will was heard,
When 'Speak for England' echoed round the House.
An ultimatum finally was sent.
No answer came. The British were at war;
And with them stood, as once before, the French.

5 Dreadnoughts and Dardanelles
Autumn 1939

This moment of impending tragedy
Brought forth, at last, the call to genius.
Churchill returned to his old offices
Within the British Board of Admiralty.
Throughout the fleet resounded now the cry,
'Winston is back!' and older men recalled
How he'd prepared the battle-fleet for war
Against the Kaiser's mighty *Kriegsmarine*.
Inside a cupboard lay the very maps
On which he'd plotted, day by day, the course
Of every ship that flew the emperor's flag.

How often then he'd spoken of the need
To build more Dreadnoughts, in excess of those
Envisaged in the German naval laws.
As he had said, it was a luxury
For Germany to have such battleships;
But, for the British, they meant life or death.
He had proposed a moratorium:
That each should stop construction for a year,
But when it was refused, he'd had no choice;
The race continued, even unto war.

What pride and admiration he had felt
For those great iron-clad monsters of the deep,
With massive guns that fired their one ton shells,
And mighty turbine engines, powered by oil,
Which he himself had bought from Persian fields
When he had overseen the change from coal.
How many days he'd passed inspecting them
At British ports from Plymouth to Rosyth.

How long he'd sat with Fisher and the rest,
In smoke-filled rooms, debating strategy.
They had abandoned any close blockade
For fear of meeting new torpedo boats.
Instead the northern seas were now patrolled
To stop the German battleships' escape
Into the vast Atlantic, where they'd roam
Across the routes of British merchantmen.
So, too, he now remembered how they'd shipped
The British army safely off to France
To fight at Mons, and later on the Marne;
And then the dreaded telegraph that told
Of British warships lost at Coronel
To von Spee's squadron; his profound relief
On hearing how the British were avenged.
He still imagined what the Germans felt
On seeing, to their uttermost surprise,
The tripod masts of Dreadnoughts in their base
Within the Falkland Islands; how they'd fled,
But soon were overhauled, and could not match
The mighty guns of British battleships.

As Churchill sat there, in that very chair
In which he'd planned the Dardanelles campaign,
His heart contracted with the bitter thoughts
Of futile carnage on those Turkish shores.
As First Lord of the Admiralty, he'd sent,
To force the passage, every ship required.
Alone they would destroy the Turkish forts,
Then sweep the minefields, cross the inner sea,
And threaten to bombard the helpless seat
Of Turkish power, the Sultan's capital.
The Black Sea would be open to the world,
The Russians saved from imminent defeat,
The Danube valley swiftly overrun.
And Allied armies on the western front
Would no more bleed their toll of youthful life.

In vain he had protested at the fears
That halted naval action in the Straits.
What were those losses, set against the deaths
Of thousand thousands on the fields of France?
And yet he'd still supported what was planned:
The seizure of the long peninsula
That held the Turks' defensive guns and forts.
Kitchener and Fisher wavered still;
The army was delayed for crucial weeks.
He'd feared the Turks would reinforce as fast
As Allied forces landed. All would turn
On rapid movement, overwhelming power.
No longer did the navy have control.
He'd argued fiercely, strove to introduce
His own conviction, energy and drive.
The soldiers had not faltered – British, French
And Anzac units left upon the shores,
Below the cliffs and wire entanglements.
Mobility was lost. Like those in France,
They'd dug their trenches, held their ground, and
     died.

Upon his shoulders fell the greatest blame
For all the errors of Gallipoli.
For he had been its strongest advocate,
The spokesman of the 'eastern strategy'.
From this disaster he had learnt one rule:
Never to be responsible again
For any task for which he lacked the power.
Dismissed from office, henceforth he was thought
A man who had no judgment. Then he'd believed
That his whole life was ruined, with no hope
That all his pent-up energy and skill
Could find a proper outlet. He'd not seen
How his beloved Clementine knew more.
She wrote to Asquith: 'Winston may have faults,
But he has what but very few possess:

The power, imagination – deadliness –
To fight the Germans.' And his own response
Was to enlist to fight them then in France.

6 The Admiralty at War
Winter 1939

Most urgent of the many weighty tasks
That bore upon him now, on his return,
Was how to meet the ever present threat
Of German U-boats. British merchant ships,
On which the life of every islander
Depended now, as always, were at risk.
Harsh memories returned of countless ships
Torpedoed in the former German war.

But counter-measures swiftly were in place.
Churchill had learnt that convoys greatly eased
The passage of the mercantile marine.
Now captains were instructed to obey
The common rules of safety, zig-zag routes
And arming of their vessels. Orders rose
For more destroyers and for trawlers, too,
Which fitted with new Asdics could detect
The prowling U-boats deep within the sea.
In vain, however, did the new First Lord
Demand control of vital Irish ports,
For Eamon de Valera still recalled
The hated Black and Tans Churchill had sent
Against the Irish rebels of Sinn Fein.

Dramatic proof was given of the skill
Of German sailors, when at Scapa Flow,
The inland harbour sheltered by the hills
Of Orkneys' islands, one bold U-boat sank
The *Royal Oak* at her moorings, with the loss
Of hundreds of her officers and men.
And German science offered further threats:

Magnetic mines below the waterline
Sank many vessels, till a way was found
To neutralise the mines' magnetic force
By means of cables girdling every ship.

Churchill was no scientist, yet he knew
How best to manage others' expertise.
He had recourse most often to his friend,
Professor Frederick Lindemann, by whom
He was informed of scientific news
That bore upon the war. Much use was made
Of figures showing trends: in shipping lost,
New output and the turnover in ports.
Demands were made by Churchill for such facts
With brusque impatience. Any brief delay
Might jeopardise some action or command.

At sea he scorned to rest upon defence.
How could he use the power of Britain's fleet
To bring to German hearts the dread of war,
And make the aggressor fear he had aroused,
From careless sleep, a new Leviathan?
His fertile mind conceived a strategy
Of startling boldness. By his naval staff
He ordered that a study should be made
Of how to send a force of battleships
Within the Baltic Sea, and threaten there
To bombard German coastlands, stop her trade,
Especially of the vital Swedish ore,
And even make a landing near Berlin.
In Baltic States the sight of British ships
Would hearten those now cowered by Germany.
Would such a stroke make Stalin hesitate
To strengthen his alliance with the Reich?
But naval experts were more sceptical:
They feared the U-boats, and lacked faith in plans
To strengthen ships against the threat of mines.
The Skagerrak might be the Dardanelles.

A second project then attracted him:
To wreck the Germans' trade upon the Rhine
With floating mines. The French objected,
Fearful lest their factories would be bombed
In swift revenge. Nor would the Cabinet
Give their full assent. Though mines were made,
They were not used before it was too late.

The members of the House were ill at ease
With Chamberlain's pursuance of the war,
And when he spoke there was but scant applause;
Whilst Churchill sat beside him on the bench,
A Chinese god of plenty, someone wrote,
With indigestion, circular and hunched.
His words were warmly greeted. With a grin,
He turned to the Prime Minister, and said:
'I have at present no conception how
This odd change in my fortunes has occurred.'
As he went on, he sounded every note
From deep concern to carefree flippancy,
From resolution to sheer boyishness,
And word by word the members' spirits rose.
For few had seen the temper of the House
So changed abruptly by a single speech.
Later they talked together in the bars:
'We have now found our leader', many said.

Meanwhile from Poland came the darkest news.
Stukas and tanks had overcome the Poles,
Whom gallantry alone could not defend
Against the *Wehrmacht*'s mechanised assault.
Churchill's broadcast strove to offer hope:
'The heroes of Warsaw are not destroyed.
The soul of Poland lives. The rock remains;
Submerged by tidal waves, it still endures.
Though Russia has pursued its interests there,
Her armies make a strong defensive front,

Which Hitler, though her ally, must deplore.
For Russia would not welcome German moves
Towards the Baltic States, nor further east.'

It fell to Churchill, once again, to rid
The sea lanes of the world of German ships.
Concealed in ocean wastes, like beasts of prey,
They struck the slow and ill-armed merchantmen.
New groups were formed to hunt the Germans down.
Into the port of Montevideo
They drove the pocket-battleship, *Graf Spee*,
Whose captain, under orders from Berlin,
Soon scuttled her, and shot himself forthwith.

Amidst the gloom of Winter, Churchill's speech,
Describing how the *Graf Spee* met her end,
Warmed British hearts with hopes of victory.
On radio his now familiar voice,
With lisping sibilants, and mocking style –
Pronouncing 'Nazi' as in 'marzipan' –
Endeared him to the people. Few could doubt
The ruthless will his irony concealed.

Royal Navy sailors, victims of *Graf Spee*,
Were held aboard the prison ship *Altmark*.
Evading all pursuers, she had reached
The fjord coast of Norway, on her way
To land the captives in a German port.
British destroyers intercepted her.
She fled to Josing fjord, seeking there,
Amidst the snow-bound slopes of vacant hills,
The safety of a neutral waterway.
But Churchill ordered *Altmark* to be searched.
A boarding party overcame the crew.
'The Navy's here!' resounded through the ship,
As British sailors clambered onto deck,
Freed from the holds of dark imprisonment.

This incident sent ripples far afield.
In England it enhanced the First Lord's claim
To prosecute the war aggressively.
In Germany it weighed on Hitler's mind.
Though pressed by Admiral Raeder, he'd preferred
That Norway should remain a neutral power.
Now Churchill's action led him to believe
That now she might submit to British plans
To occupy her ports, and interrupt
The flow of iron ore from the Swedish fields,
Upon which German armaments relied.

This latter scheme, indeed, had long appealed
To Churchill's judgment. When the war began
He had considered how the Swedish ore
Could be denied to German industry.
In Winter, when the northern Baltic froze,
It was supplied from Narvik, down the coast,
Through neutral waters, safely to the Reich.
If these were mined, the ore-ships would be forced
To enter seas patrolled by British ships.
Persistently had Churchill made the case
That rights of smaller countries should not count
Against those measures from which all would gain.
Without the iron their armaments required,
The Germans could not much prolong the war.

Should moral scruples jeopardise those lives
Which would be lost on future battlefields?
But, in the British Cabinet, Churchill's voice,
Demanding action, eager to engage,
Had failed to move the scruples and the doubts
Of those same men, who not so long before,
Had hailed, in vain, the Munich settlement.

The Russians meanwhile had attacked the Finns
To gain more ground for Leningrad's defence.

Though Finnish bravery was much admired,
And many people favoured Allied moves
To go to their assistance, Churchill said
The main objective should be Swedish ore.
In London and in Paris long debates
Took place upon this issue. Plans were made
For Allied landings at Norwegian ports,
Anticipating Germany's response.
Yet nothing was decided. Churchill watched,
Frustrated at the lack of leadership.
In France Edouard Daladier resigned;
To be replaced by Reynaud, one inclined
To fight the war with more audacity.
But still, in England, Chamberlain remained;
Although, when people talked about the war
In offices and factories, shops or streets,
The name of Churchill was upon their lips.

Affronted by the *Altmark* incident,
The *Führer* now accepted Raeder's view
That holding Norway furthered German aims.
By sea and air the *Wehrmacht* would descend
Upon Norwegian ports and aerodromes.
The basic aim, his War Directive said,
Was that the *Wehrmacht* should appear to come
As mere protectors of Norwegian rights.
And yet surprise was vital. Any means
To break down all resistance would be used.
This *Operation Weser* would precede
The opening of offensives in the west.
Both surface ships and submarines could hide
Along the fjord coast. British blockade
Would be no more a threat; and Swedish ore
Would be secured throughout the Winter months.

So when at last the Cabinet gave assent
To mining the Norwegian waterways

And landings to begin at Narvik port,
They found the Germans had forestalled them there,
At Oslo and at other major ports.
This was a bitter blow to Churchill's pride.
How had the German navy carried there,
To Norway's western coast, those *Wehrmacht* troops,
Without alerting Britain's northern fleet?
The Narvik force had briefly been observed
By air reconnaissance. The Admiralty,
Not realising how bold the *Führer* was,
Did not believe that Narvik was their goal.

Belatedly the British navy fought
To compensate, by courage, for its lack
Of necessary vigilance and speed.
Along the fjord coast fierce actions flamed
Between the British and the *Kriegsmarine*.
The German losses so reduced their fleet
That when, weeks later, Britain faced the threat
Of mass invasion from the Channel ports,
The German generals feared to cross the sea.

When, in the Commons, Churchill rose to speak,
He looked quite tired, and hesitated much
In fumbling with his notes and spectacles.
He could not really say how it occurred
That German ships arrived at Narvik first.
But later, in the Cabinet, he urged
That Narvik, first of all, must be regained.
The prime objective still remained the same:
To halt the flow of ore to German ports.

Yet other views prevailed. The case was made
For taking Trondheim, further to the south.
So Allied forces sailed to Namsos, too,
And Aandalsnes, to make a pincer move
From north and south on Trondheim's garrison.

Disaster followed. Under air attack
And ill-equipped to move in heavy snow,
They gave some help to Norway's patriots,
But then returned to havens on the coast.
Theirs was the first of many such retreats.

Whilst long delay ensued at Narvik port,
Despite the First Lord's plea of urgency,
On mainland Europe mightier events
Cast Norway's tragic battle into shade,
And left its sturdy people and its land
To traitors and the will of Germany.
Deficient in equipment, poorly led,
And hamstrung by political neglect,
The Allied forces soon withdrew by sea.
This was a bitter foretaste of defeat
In other theatres at the *Wehrmacht*'s hands.
Though Narvik had been stormed belatedly,
It could not now be held. The German grip
On Norway's vital coastline was complete.

7 Prime Minister at Last
Spring 1940

Now Chamberlain, like Asquith once before,
Was faced by angry critics, those who saw
Delay and indecision, lack of will
To implement a war-like policy.
Within the House of Commons fierce debates
Revealed his government's loss of confidence.
Loud cheers rang out at Cromwell's quoted words:
'You've sat too long for any good you've done.
Depart, I say, let us have done with you.
Go, in the name of God!' Then Churchill spoke,
And took upon himself whatever blame
Might fall upon the navy for its part.
For he would not play traitor to the man
Whom he'd agreed to serve, whatever doubts
He harboured secretly. The risk was great –
Would Norway be a new Gallipoli
That cast fresh doubts upon his competence?

On this occasion wiser voices rose
To rescue Churchill from the government's fall.
For all remembered how he had appealed
For proper measures to enhance defence;
How he'd foreseen the dire calamity
That threatened England now. Yet even he
Could not protect the government from defeat.
So when a large majority was lost,
Its fate was settled. Also Chamberlain knew
He could not form a National government,
For Labour did not want his leadership.

The aging Premier, sick at heart and ill,
Departed from the Chamber, knowing now

That all that he had stood for, all his work
To compromise with Hitler, and to save
Great Britain and the world from total war,
Had come to nothing. His sole recompense
Was but to serve with what strength still remained.

Who then would succeed him? – Halifax?
Upright, unblemished, English to the core,
Indifferent to the siren call of fame,
More suited to diplomacy than war,
The natural choice of most Conservatives?
Or one who never was a party man,
But rather a most skilled antagonist
In warfare and debate, a man marked out
For bold endeavours, eager for the fight,
Who once engaged would rarely compromise?
Yet one who roused suspicion. Who would trust –
To such a maverick – the nation's fate?

The cup was offered them by Chamberlain.
For once the First Lord did not choose to speak.
Then Halifax, aware he was not cast
For such a role in times climacteric,
Gave reasons why a peer should not succeed.
He would have power without the right to speak
In that assembly on whose full support
All British governments must perforce rely.
Churchill did not demur. The die was cast.

Buckingham Palace summoned him forthwith.
'Do you know why you've come?' enquired the King.
'I simply can't imagine', Churchill quipped;
But, with due reverence, kissed the monarch's hand.
In unaccustomed silence, he returned,
With his detective, to the Admiralty.
'How great the task you have!' the policeman said.
'God only knows how great', was the reply.
'I fear it is too late. We'll do our best.'

He had not been surprised. He later wrote:
'For I was conscious of profound relief.
At last I had authority to give
Directions over all the scene of war.
I felt as if I walked with destiny,
That all my life prepared me for this hour.
For years I had been free from party strife.
Were not my warnings vindicated now?
None could gainsay me. None could ever claim
That I had made the war; nor could they say
That I, indeed, was unprepared for it.
I thought I knew a good deal of it all,
And I was sure that I would never fail.
Impatient for the morning, I slept well.
Why should I dream? The facts were quite enough!'

The time was apposite for such a change.
The House of Commons, blessed with prescience,
Foresaw the most severe of crises faced
By those who'd lived within the British Isles.
For now the great assault, so long withheld,
Broke forth upon the western allies' front.
On Holland, Belgium, France the storm clouds burst.
To countryside and towns oft swept by war,
Where Marlborough and Napoleon had fought,
Where modern armies three decades before
Had scorched the earth, and left a wilderness,
Now came the flood of armies mechanised
And airborne weapons deadly in effect.

Churchill's government speedily was formed.
In such a crisis most were quick to serve,
And party differences were overborne.
Yet in the House of Commons some were loth
To welcome him as leader. Many felt
He was unbalanced, too ambitious, rash,
Not quite a gentleman. Were not his friends,

Like Beaverbrook and Bracken, dangerous men?
Indeed, the House gave Chamberlain more cheers
Than Churchill got, when first he entered there
To speak of his new government's policy.

'Nothing I have to offer', he proclaimed,
'Except for blood, and toil and tears and sweat.
You ask, "What is our policy?". I say:
To wage a war by sea and land and air
With all the might and strength that God can give,
To wage a war 'gainst monstrous tyranny,
Unparalleled in catalogues of crime.
You ask, "What is our aim?" I answer thus:
At all cost, victory, in spite of all,
However long and hard the road may be.
Without our victory, we will not survive;
The British Empire will not then survive,
And all it stands for. Nor will there survive
The urge and impulse of our history,
And mankind's movement to its proper goal.
But I take up my task with buoyant hope,
In certainty our cause will never fail.
I feel the right to claim the aid of all.
Let us go forward with united strength.'

Later, General Ismay walked with him
From Downing Street, beside Horse Guards Parade,
Where, in the Park, the springtime blossom shone.
Some people stood outside the Admiralty.
'Good luck, God bless you, Winnie', many cried.
Inside the building, he dissolved in tears.
'So these poor people trust me, yet for long
There's nothing but disaster I can give.'

8 The Battle of France
Spring 1940

Neutral Belgium could not be induced
To welcome Allied armies in her land,
Lest they should rouse the wrath of Germany.
Instead the Allies manned the borderline,
From near Dunkirk to where the French had built
The Maginot Line as far as Switzerland.
But now the fierce attack of German arms
Upon their homeland raised the Belgian cry
For urgent help to stem the sudden tide.
No word from Winston Churchill was required.
The plan was made: the British forces drove
Through welcoming towns, with belfries newly built,
Where people ran to shake the tommies' hands;
And past the level fields of growing corn,
Near where their kin had held the bloody lines
Of Ypres and Menin, Loos and Vimy Ridge,
To man defences on the River Dyle.

In Holland swift disaster was in train.
The Dutch had planned to bar the way with floods,
But *Stuka* planes and elite paratroops
Soon overstepped the inundated land.
All fighting ceased when Rotterdam was bombed
And gutted streets proclaimed the cost of war.
So, too, in Belgium paratroops had struck,
Taking Eban Emael, a crucial fort,
And bridges on the Albert waterway.
Stubbornly the British held their ground,
But further south the French were faltering.

Hitler had approved a German plan
To concentrate his armour at the point

Where French defences were most tenuous.
This lay in the Ardennes, whose wooded hills
And steep-cut valleys seemed a natural wall
Against the rapid movement of a force
Of tanks and guns and soldiers motorised.

But here the *Wehrmacht* proved itself supreme
In skilful preparation, and the choice
Of bold commanders, set on victory.
Soon they were on the Meuse, their vanguard force,
Composed of panzers, eager to advance.
Too late the French opposed their river boats
And engineers, who built a bridge at Glaire.
When, at Sedan and Montcornet, they'd crossed,
Before them lay the plains of Picardie,
Where tanks could freely range. Five days of war
Had deeply wounded France. German armour,
Seeking every gap, now flowed like water
Through her infantry. All unity was lost.
A dagger's thrust had left her speechless,
Lacking all command. Grave thoughts were stirring.
Men laid down their arms. The bravest died;
And those in power saw imminent collapse.

When, early in the morning, Reynaud rang,
He spoke in English, clearly under stress;
'The battle has been lost. It is defeat.'
Churchill responded: 'Surely not so soon?'
'The front is broken, broken near Sedan;
The tanks pour through, so many', Reynaud said.
'The road is open. Paris will be lost.'

'The German breakthrough on a narrow front',
Said Churchill slowly, 'cannot penetrate.
It cannot be exploited rapidly.
Remember now the twenty-first of March
In that last year of war. They had to halt
To gather their supplies. The chance had come

To cut off their attack. From Foch himself
I learned this at the time. So is it now.
The Germans will be vulnerable again.'

'But we have lost the battle', Reynaud said.
'We beg for your assistance. Send more troops.
You have so few at present here in France.'
'No help from us could come in time to change
The outcome of this battle', Churchill said;
'But I must add, whatever France may do,
We shall not stop. We will fight on alone.'

He was prepared to go to Paris then
And talk about the crisis, face to face.
That very afternoon, an unarmed plane,
A small Flamingo, carried him to France.
Arriving at Le Bourget, he was told
The Germans were expected within days.

But on the streets of Paris no one knew
How dire the crisis was. The shops were busy,
Bars and cafes full. Wine glasses clinked
On marble table tops, and even artists
Still sat patiently, along the quays
Below the Notre Dame. The headlines read
Of valiant defence, and nothing yet
Was heard of refugees; though Belgian cars
Were seen more often on the boulevards.

But, at the Quai d'Orsay, an air of gloom
Pervaded now the gilded room of State,
Where Churchill met the Ministers of France.
All were dejected. Gamelin began
By showing on a map what had occurred.
Behind Sedan, the black line of the front
Depicted clearly where the breach was made.
After the armour, Gamelin foretold,

The motorised divisions would advance
To reinforce the German corridor.
The French commander stopped. There was a pause.

Then Churchill asked, 'Where are the main reserves?'
Gamelin turned, and slowly shook his head.
'*Aucune*', he said. There was another pause,
Whilst through the windows of the Quai d'Orsay,
They all could see the clouds of smoke that rose,
Like auguries of war, from garden fires,
As documents were burnt, archives and files,
By foreign office staff. In Churchill's mind
Two thoughts were dominant: that German tanks
Could penetrate so far, and that the French,
The mighty army of the former war,
Whose *poilus* in their millions had been drawn
From every corner of their native soil
To drive the dread invaders from the land,
Had nothing in reserve to bring to bear.
Where were the troops to strike the German flanks,
And cut the lifelines of their armoured thrust?

There was some talk of how to gather strength,
With fresh divisions to attack the bulge.
But Gamelin had lost the will to fight:
'Inferior in numbers, guns and tanks,
Inferior in method!' – then he shrugged.
And yet he pleaded, as Reynaud had done,
For British fighter aircraft – Hurricanes –
To stop the tanks. But Churchill disagreed:
'The guns should stop the armour, not the planes.
They cleanse the sky above the battlefield.'

And yet, that night, he sent a telegram
To ask the Cabinet for six squadrons more.
'We must provide air cover for the French
To have a final chance to show their strength.

If our refusal leads to their collapse,
Then history is our judge.' They answered 'yes'.

He took the news to Reynaud's Paris flat.
It was in darkness. In the sitting room,
Comtesse de Portes' fur coat lay on a chair.
Reynaud appeared, and, in his dressing-gown,
He listened to what Churchill read aloud –
His telegram and London's swift reply.
They sent a man to fetch Daladier.
He did not speak a word, but crossed the room
And grasped the British Premier by the hand.
Then Churchill tried to summon up resolve
In both the Frenchmen, by a fierce harangue.
Brandishing his cigar, he paced the room,
As they sat listening, one bowed down with grief,
The other also silent, but erect.

Air Chief Marshal Dowding, in command
Of Britain's fighter forces, wrote that day
To emphasise his view that no more planes
Should fly to France, however great the need.
'If home defence is drained away', he wrote,
'To remedy the desperate state of France,
Then her undoing means for us the same,
Complete and irremediable defeat.'

That evening Reynaud broadcast to the French,
Insisting that their troops were fighting hard,
And that the government did not mean to leave.
'It is in Paris; there it will remain.'
And yet he warned his colleagues to prepare
To go, if needs be, to Algeria,
And carry on the war from overseas.

Churchill returned to London. Paul Reynaud,
Determined to fight on, appointed now

The aged General Weygand in command,
A seemingly efficient officer,
Who'd served as Chief of Staff to Marshal Foch.
A bold plan was devised. From Amiens
A new French army, formed from diverse groups,
Would cut the line of panzers from the south,
Whilst British forces, with the neighbouring French,
Attacking down towards the River Somme,
Would meet them near Cambrai. The German tanks
Which threatened now to reach the Channel ports,
Would be disrupted, halting their advance.

Once more in Paris, Churchill met Weygand,
And gave support to his initiative.
But yet, he added, as an afterthought,
That General Gort, whilst fighting to Cambrai,
Must still maintain his pathway to the sea.
Meanwhile the roads were choked with refugees
And French deserters, laying down their arms.

Churchill brought to London words of hope
That Weygand's plan would turn the tide of war,
But in his heart he knew what might impend:
The fall of France and doom of British arms.
Yet to his staff and colleagues, as he worked,
Beset by Cabinet boxes, telegrams
And many callers, most with dismal news,
His face exuded confidence and strength.
He puffed at his cigar, and sipped a drink,
Quite calm amidst a myriad of cares.
His very presence countenanced no fear;
His voice inspired; his speech moved men to act
With no regard for personal consequence.

The French attack from Amiens was weak;
Nor could the British break out from Arras.
A crucial choice was made by Gort himself.

Abandoning his drive towards the south,
He turned his forces back towards the sea.
On Churchill's desk lay Reynaud's fierce complaint,
But it was clear that Weygand's plan had failed.
General Gort's decision was endorsed;
And Churchill knew the war in France was lost.

9 Dunkirk
Spring 1940

Already plans were made for naval ships
And many others, every kind of craft,
To bring the army home from Channel ports.
Boulogne had fallen. Calais was besieged.
Churchill ordered, to his own dismay,
The garrison to fight until the end
To hold the panzers back for days or hours,
Whilst Allied forces fortified Dunkirk.

In Britain life continued untoward.
The parks in London blossomed in the Sun.
The West End shops were busy; theatres showed
Their pre-war entertainments. At weekends
A calmness still pervaded city streets.
There was no fear, but much anxiety.
The people did not know the full extent
Of what their army faced across the sea:
Encirclement and absolute defeat.
Nor did they know what bitter words were said
Behind closed doors in Cabinet arguments.

For Churchill did not govern unopposed.
In Downing Street five Ministers of war,
The inner Cabinet, sat in conference.
The long, high room, with vacant leather chairs
And tall Corinthian pillars, clocks and phones,
Looked almost empty, slightly dark within;
But through the shuttered windows they could see,
In brilliant sunshine, plane trees in the Park,
And sentries posted on Horse Guards Parade.

Churchill, Attlee, Greenwood, Chamberlain
And Halifax, the Foreign Secretary,
Discussed at length what options now remained.
Lord Halifax, of these, was most inclined
To look for terms from Hitler. He proposed
They ask the Italian government for its help.
Would Mussolini make a settlement,
With honour for the chief belligerents?
Yet all suspected Italy was close
To stabbing France to gain the spoils of war.
But Halifax persisted: 'Why not now
Agree to terms that do not threaten us;
That leave us independent as a State?'

Churchill opposed him: 'Do we trust again
The word of Hitler, whilst we are so weak?
If we stop fighting, what will he demand?
We would concede that Europe should be left
To Nazi domination; that we leave
The lives of Frenchmen, Belgians and the Dutch –
And Poles, for whom we first engaged in war –
To be determined by Herr Hitler's will.
And what then of our own security?
Our only choice, our only safe recourse,
Is to convince him that we are resolved;
That he cannot defeat us; that alone.'

Debate continued, passionate but cool.
This was no time for personal enmity.
All knew the life of Britain was at stake.
Attlee and Greenwood favoured Churchill's view.
Would Chamberlain, who'd striven hard for peace,
Now give support to Halifax's scheme?
They were old colleagues, both Conservatives,
The men of Munich, eager to appease.
If they resigned, then Churchill could be doomed.
Too many men still thought him dangerous,
A man of war, a rash adventurer.

But Chamberlain had changed. He was not well.
Throughout his efforts to avert this war,
Incurable illness slowly had advanced.
Hitler had deceived him. Not again
Would he be led by wishful hopes of peace,
When everything proclaimed the need for war.
He'd worked with Churchill, seen his strength of will,
His utter resolution to succeed,
Not for himself, but for his nation's cause.
To one another each had been most loyal.
Their roles had been reversed, yet neither now
Resented what was past. A common aim,
To save the world from Hitler, guided them.

Halifax was defeated. He had sought
To end the war by reasoned compromise.
The 'Holy Fox', as Churchill labelled him,
Was not ambitious. He did not conspire
To take the reins of power from Churchill's hands.
He had refused the task; he was most loyal,
A Christian servant of his high ideals,
Conservative, peace-loving, reasonable.
But he'd not learnt, as Chamberlain had done,
That Hitler was unreason's champion.

Was Churchill now secure in his resolve
To carry on, whatever were the odds?
The inner Cabinet had supported him,
But what of others, now the country knew
That Britain's army was in full retreat,
That France might be defeated? Who could tell
What fear and panic might engulf the land?
A Home Guard had been formed, but ill equipped.
How many planes had been shot down in France?
The navy was still strong, but rumours ran
Of German parachutists, and the threat
Of massive bombing by the *Luftwaffe*.

Wider support was needed, so he called
All members of the Cabinet to his room
To hear a statement which he had prepared.
He said whatever happened at Dunkirk
We would fight on, and to his own surprise,
They cheered and ran to him and shook his hand.
Their sentiments were his, nor could he doubt
The mood within the country; for these men
Still represented their constituents,
Men of all parties, now of common voice.
He was, this moment, unassailable.

Again he flew to Paris, where he met
The aged Marshal Petain, with Reynaud.
Fresh plans were made to strike at Italy,
And at Dunkirk arrangements would ensue
For French and British both to be embarked.
The strategy of Reynaud was to hold
A strengthened line along the River Somme.
Churchill said that, even if France fell,
The British would not come to any terms.
Even from the New World they would fight.
But Marshal Petain, in civilian clothes,
Appeared detached and sombre. Would he make,
So Churchill asked himself, a separate peace?

The British navy, aided by a host
Of little private ships from southern ports,
Brought back the army from the Dunkirk shore.
They left behind their tanks and heavy guns.
The Germans had delayed their own advance,
In case of danger to their armoured force
From streams and ditches in the hinterland.
Was Hitler also fearing to destroy
The imperial power of Britain? Europe stood
Prostrate before him. Why not then permit
Another German race to dominate

The inferior peoples of the wider world?
In any case, the *Luftwaffe* could bomb
The homeland British till they would submit.

When only wreckage lay on Dunkirk beach,
Then Churchill spoke of this deliverance.
Dressed in black, and looking rather stout,
With gestures now familiar to the House –
Smoothing his waistcoat, patting down his chest –
He told how much the army was deprived
Of everything, except the men themselves.
'For their survival highest praise is due
To sailors who have braved the bombs and mines,
And also to the air force, who have fought
Above, and far beyond, the threatened shores.
This augurs well for battles in the air,
When this, our island, is itself attacked.
Yet though we should rejoice at what is done,
This saving grace is not a victory.
Evacuations do not win a war.
Hitler plans to invade the British Isles.
Without delay we must be re-equipped.
In England now we are not short of men.
Napoleon was told of bitter weeds
That lay in wait for his invasion force.
There are far more, with our return from France.
Though old and famous States are in the grip
Of Nazi rule – Gestapo and the rest –
We shall not flag nor fail. We shall go on
And fight until the end; upon the seas;
Especially in the air. At any cost,
We will defend our land, upon our shores,
On landing-grounds and fields, in city streets,
And in the farthest hills. We shall fight on,
And not surrender, never, come what may!
And even if we're finally destroyed,
Our British Empire, guarded by the fleet,

Will still pursue the struggle, till the time,
When all the New World's power and energy
Will come at last to liberate the Old.'

It was a speech, so one observer said,
Of fine Elizabethan phrases. 'One could feel
A massive power behind them, and resolve,
Like a great fortress, built behind the words.'

Even whilst the final soldiers came,
Phlegmatic in defeat, to Britain's ports,
Their leader, Churchill, contemplated how
To save the French from imminent collapse.
Enigma decrypts told of German plans
To conquer France before they would invade.
Hence he proposed to reinforce the French
With fresh divisions, all those still equipped,
And make a redoubt, perhaps in Brittany.

Meanwhile, in England, work increased apace,
To build defences, train new volunteers,
Imprison aliens and root out spies,
And labour with a new intensity
To manufacture arms of every sort,
Replacing those abandoned, making more,
To give the forces weapons of offence.
Already from the U.S.A. there came
The rifles, guns and ammunition stocks,
Which he'd requested from the President.

For though, in office, Churchill had become
More circumspect, less rash, and quick to learn
From others' views and expert evidence,
He still remained aggressive, never prone
To follow where the enemy had led.
The fire that spurred him on at Omdurman,
That drove him from Pretoria's prison camp,

That urged him to demand an eastern front,
Far off in Turkey at the Dardanelles,
That burned within him, even when he'd fought
In Ploegstreet's trenches, deep in mire and blood,
Had not abated. Now it smouldered on,
Awaiting that due time when it would blaze,
Consuming those who now confined its flames.

For many English people, it felt strange
To have no sense of what the future held,
Of what, in hours, might suddenly befall.
'This ignorance', said one, 'is now acute.
I see what is to come in garish terms,
In lurid shades of scarlet and of black.'

10 The Agony of France
Summer 1940

Another meeting with the French was due,
For every day brought darker news from France.
Reynaud's government was en route for Tours,
As German armour closed upon the Seine.
Once more in his Flamingo, Churchill flew –
This time amidst a swarm of Hurricanes –
To meet the French at Briare on the Loire.
The airfield was deserted. One man came
To take them to Chateau de Muguet,
Where Reynaud, Weygand, Vuillemin and Petain
Awaited them with ill-concealed despair.
Only de Gaulle looked calm and confident.

Weygand described the French predicament.
He seemed intent on showing all was lost.
The long defensive line from east to west
Was thinly manned and breached at many points.
Troops were exhausted, short of food and sleep,
Demoralised by constant air attack.
The German armour spearheads went unchecked.
The roads were choked by crowds of refugees,
Bewildered, lost, machine-gunned from the air.
In days, or hours, Parisians would see
The soldiers of the Reich on city streets.
The sibilant voice of Weygand rose a pitch.
'Now I am helpless. I can't intervene.
This is the break-up. There are no reserves.'

The British, even Churchill, were aghast
At such a tale of unrelieved defeat.
They asked for confirmation. Alphonse Georges,

A trusted general, offered no more hope.
Was this the army Churchill once had seen
As valiant bayonets winning rights of man,
And standing guard of Europe's liberties?
There was a pause; then Churchill spoke himself,
With slow, deliberate words of confidence.
'It is a matter', he assured the French,
'Of hanging on, whilst new reserves are found.
British and Canadians will come
To join the French within a few short weeks.
Is this not like the battle of the Marne,
When France was saved by seeming miracles,
Or like when Marshal Petain had recoiled
Upon the Hun offensive near Beauvais?
Already British aircraft are at work
From aerodromes in France, incessantly.
This crisis will not last. The time will come
When fresh reserves of men and weaponry,
From England's Empire and America,
Will reinforce the Allies here in France,
And turn the course of history. So I believe.'

Weygand was unimpressed. 'There is no time
To wait for reinforcements. All will turn
Upon this final quarter of an hour.
Once Paris falls, there will be nothing left
To stop the Germans taking all our towns.
Then any fighting will not be controlled.
As French Commander I will have no power.
How then can France continue with the war?'

Reynaud was angry at these final words.
His eyebrows arched, his eyes looked furious.
'Government alone shall make the final choice
Of when the war should end.' Weygand replied,
Sarcastically, that he would gladly serve
Whoever could escape from this debacle.

Closely watching this internal feud,
The British leader offered, once again
Some further prospects to prolong the war.
Would not Paris, as Madrid had done,
Entangle its assailants like a maze,
Absorb their armies, paralyse their tanks,
And immolate their soldiers in its fires?
A picture was presented of the glow
Of burning cities – Athens, Rome, Madrid –
Of lovely buildings crushing friends and foes,
Of garrisons, who would not see defeat,
All lying dead in smoking monuments.
At such an image every Frenchman froze.

Then Petain spoke, his face a mask of stone,
His bony hands spread out expressively.
'When soldiers rallied in the former war,
I had fresh units ready to attack.'
He paused, then added in a bitter tone,
'A million British then were in the line.
Cities of ruins, Paris or the rest,
Will not affect the issue of the war.'
Unknown to Churchill, Weygand had declared
That Paris was to be an open town,
With no defences, even at the forts,
Nor blowing up of bridges on the Seine.

Persistently the British leader asked
About an Allied bridgehead in the west.
Brittany could be a strong redoubt,
Until new forces, landed from the sea,
Would drive the Germans out. Guerilla war,
Meanwhile, throughout the country, would ensure
That *Wehrmacht* soldiers never would be safe,
Their lives tormented. Could the Nazis hold
So many nations in their murderous grip,
Whilst fighting still in France and on the seas?

The French were adamant. How could they make
A bridgehead in the west without reserves,
When all their troops were fighting or were trapped?
In Brittany there were no industries.
The rest of France would pay a heavy price,
A hostage at the mercy of the Reich.
What had they done in Poland and elsewhere?
Even Georges could offer no support
To his old comrade, Britain's Premier.

De Gaulle, uniquely, gave encouragement
By asking that the lighter British tanks
Should join armoured units of the French
To give them help with their reconnaissance.
He also was entrusted with the task
Of studying a plan for Brittany.
The British party saw in him alone –
This tall, impassive Frenchman – some fresh spark,
Amidst the dying glow of Gallic arms.

One vital issue stood to be resolved.
Before they left for France, the British chiefs
Had heard their leader bow to expert views
That Britain's air defences could not spare
More fighter squadrons for the war in France.
Air Marshal Dowding had insisted on
Withholding fighters for the crucial time
When Goering's planes would bomb the British Isles.
Now Churchill faced at Briare desperate men,
United in their one convulsive cry
For help with aircraft. This alone could save
Their failing army. With more air support
They would withstand the guns and infantry,
Even the deadly panzers, once relieved
Of *Stuka* bombs, of terror from the air.
'This the decisive moment, this the point
At which to concentrate our every force,

According to the principles of war.
The battle can be turned, if you will send
To France today your pilots and your planes.'

All eyes were turned on Churchill. All well knew
His love for France, his memory of the times
When he had seen her soldiers' sacrifice
To save the world from German dominance.
He knew the pride and honour of the French,
Their comradeship in arms, their cultured life.
Could he decline the hand of friendship now,
Whilst he beheld their hour of agony?

He did not hesitate. He did not yield
The power of reason to his sympathy.
'This is not now the one decisive point.
That moment comes when Hitler gives the word
To send the German air force on our shores.
If we retain command of our own air,
And keep the oceans open, then in time,
In God's good time, we'll win all back for you.
We shall fight on, for ever, everywhere,
And without mercy, until victory.'

Before they left Briare, Churchill had said
To Jean Darlan, Commander of the Fleet,
'Don't let it ever fall in German hands.'
And solemnly the Admiral gave his word.

They flew back by Flamingo. Due to cloud,
There was no escort, and above the sea
Were German fighters, hunting fishing boats.
They were not spotted, and came safely home.

Within a day an urgent call came through
To summon Churchill once again to France.
For, at Briare, Reynaud had promised him

To let him know of an emergency.
In London now –a warm and sunny day –
The Summer crowds ill knew the present threat
From Hitler's armies on the further shore,
And German bombers on French aerodromes.

At Tours they landed on a cratered strip.
No one met them. In a borrowed car
They drove unguided to the Prefecture.
Churchill was greeted by his friend, Mandel,
One whom he trusted never to renege,
But who would be betrayed by weaker men.

When Reynaud spoke, the state of France was clear.
The army was prostrate – at its last gasp.
An armistice might be their next recourse.
The only hope lay with America.
He thus proposed to send to Roosevelt
A message that the final hour had come.
A firm assurance of immediate aid
Alone could save them; for his colleagues said,
Why carry on when all that can result
Is German occupation? Then he paused,
And looked embarrassed, unaccustomedly.
'Will Britain now release France from her pledge
That she would not conclude a separate peace?
Already France has sacrificed herself.
Nothing is left. That is the awful truth.'
He stopped, and sat awaiting a response.

Reynaud himself had changed. Diminutive,
But animated, cheerful, quick to act,
Expressive, optimistic, keen to find
A way through any problem – now he looked
Somewhat evasive, hesitant, unsure,
As though he spoke for others, those who thought
That compromise with Hitler must be found,

Like Baudouin, who sat in silence there,
And absent figures – Weygand and Petain –
Whose ominous shades now sullied every word
That Reynaud uttered. Others, too, had changed.

No longer were there allies in a war.
A rift had opened. Nations were at stake.
Their friendship still remained, but now each saw
A parting of the ways, a subtle break;
For each must serve his cause. And Churchill, too,
Though still most sympathetic, looked intent
On weighing all that Paul Reynaud had said
To find within it how the French would act.
No mention had been made, as once before,
Of Reynaud's will to fight in Africa.

Then Churchill answered: 'Britain is aware
How France has suffered. Soon our turn will come.
We grieve our contribution is so small,
Yet we have followed Allied strategy
In fighting on the northern battlefields.
Henceforth we have but one impelling thought:
To rid the world of Hitler; that one aim.
The British can endure; they will persist.
If France keeps fighting on beyond the sea,
We will gain time. America may come
To give the Allies overwhelming strength.
The other course means France will be destroyed,
For Hitler does not honour any pledge.
At all events, Great Britain will fight on.
No terms and no surrender. She will fight
For death or victory. That is my reply.'

His voice despondent, Reynaud pleaded still.
'It is too late to fight in Brittany.
There is no place in France where we can stay –
The present government – out of German hands.

And if we leave, then Hitler will be free
To set up puppets, Quislings, in our stead.
Why can we not conclude a separate peace,
And yet maintain our ancient amity?'
It was a final offer of despair.
And Reynaud's voice betrayed his disbelief.

'We will not make reproaches', Churchill said,
'Bu neither will we give your our consent
To any peace that contravenes your pledge.'

A note was passed to Churchill. Would he stop
To give the British moments to confer?
They walked outside. The garden was still wet
From heavy rain, but now the sky had cleared.
They slowly paced the rectangle of green,
Avoiding pools of water and the leaves
Of dripping laurels, glistening in the Sun.
All were agreed that France must keep her pledge,
But Beaverbrook now urged a telegram
Be sent forthwith to Franklin Roosevelt;
For only his support could hearten France.

Meanwhile the French themselves were arguing;
As Georges Mandel, Jeanneney and Heriot
Opposed most strongly any armistice,
And Reynaud was rebuked for his idea
Of asking England to release the French.

The meeting was resumed. De Gaulle had come.
His brooding figure watched with hooded eyes,
As Churchill said the British were agreed
On not consenting to a separate peace.
But Renault's mood had altered. Unperturbed,
He said he would appeal to Roosevelt,
And turning then to Churchill, he avowed
That when they met again they would discuss

The ways and means of fighting Germany.
A paradox arose in British minds:
Had Reynaud been assessing their resolve
And, reassured, was once more confident?

The British thanked him, and prepared to leave,
But Winston Churchill raised a final point,
Which showed how strong his reservations were.
Hundreds of German pilots were in France
As prisoners of war. Could they be sent
At once to England? Reynaud gave his word;
But soon he would be powerless to comply.
As Churchill later wrote, with irony,
'We had to shoot them down a second time.'

De Gaulle was at the doorway when they left.
Churchill looked up at him, and said in French,
'*L'homme du destin*', barely audibly.
The General stood apparently unmoved.
Then just as Churchill got into his car,
Comtesse de Portes, the mistress of Reynaud,
Pushed forward from the waiting dignitaries,
And shouted to him, 'You must hear me speak.
My country bleeds to death. You must hear me.'
He shut the door, as though he had not heard.
For she was Reynaud's evil counsellor.

Meanwhile, at Cangey, other Ministers
Awaited with unease the news from Tours.
They thought that Reynaud would bring Churchill
    there,
And when they heard he'd flown home again
They felt that England had abandoned them.
Vexation, anger, and – for some – relief,
Now swayed their judgment. Few henceforth could find
Reserves of strength to struggle on alone.
Who now opposed the swelling cries for peace?

70

Why had he left? None had invited him.
He could not ask, himself, to meet these men.
Thus was the Sun of France so soon eclipsed.

m.
e you well
do admire.
ults.
ry.'
gnature –
a pig.

rength
frica
es de Gaulle.
nce,

l of France,
d defence,
ight.
larion call.
ly to France.

ranged
States.
him off.
oo;
sage came:
Bordeaux,
uld be
mier.
nion.
ught
onies.
red,
ishmen.
d you prefer
eich,
mmonwealth?'
to resign.
th the task

11 Armistice
Summer 1940

With France in torment, Churchill sent a p[
Supporting Reynaud, to the President.
His prompt reply made offers of supplies,
But could not promise war. Only Congress
Had the lawful power. When Churchill aske[
To publish this response, he was refused.

Meanwhile, Paris, undefended, fell.
Along the Champs Elysees, Germans marche[
Triumphantly beneath the swastika.
Far to the east, the line of Maginot
Was taken in the rear. The arms of France
On every front, were broken and dispersed,
And British troops imperilled in the west.

Churchill spoke by telephone to Brooke,
Insisting that they still should serve the Frencl[
But Brooke was adamant: 'We cannot help
To bring a corpse to life; the French are dead!'
For half an hour they argued, till at last
The soldiers' case was won. The order came,
'Evacuate them all from Normandy'.
Four years later some of them returned.

To Roosevelt a further text was sent:
'In this dark hour, when Britain fights alone,
I must remind you of what this implies.
If we are beaten – which I don't foresee –
Then with a feeble Quisling government,
The British fleet would be the only means
Of buying better terms from Germany.

Urbanity and kindness, and be ca[
I cannot bear that those who serv[
Should not now love you, as they[
Anger and rudeness do not get res[
They either breed dislike, or slave[
She sketched a cat beneath her si[
A private emblem. Winston's was[

A final gesture to give Reynaud s[
To keep the French at war from A[
Was made on the advice of Charl[
A declaration would be sent at o[
Proposing an undying union
Between the States of Britain and[
With common citizens, and share[
To carry on the war with all its m[
'Then we shall conquer!' was its [
De Gaulle would take it personal[

And once again a meeting was a[
Between the leaders of the allied[
Churchill's wife had come to see[
He waited in the train at Waterl[
But there was some delay. A mes[
Reynaud's government, sitting a[
Was in a state of crisis. There w[
No meeting with the British Pre[
Nor would the French consider [
Led by Marshal Petain, many th[
It was a trick to seize French col[
To be a Nazi province, one decl[
Was better than the rule of Eng[
To which Mandel replied: 'Wou[
To be a subject of the German [
Or dwell within the British Co[
Yet Reynaud had no choice but[
Petain formed a government, w[

Of asking for an armistice forthwith.
De Gaulle escaped to England in a plane.

Along the many boulevards of France
The shadows darkened. On the battlefields
The guns were silent, but in every heart
Awakening fears displaced the sounds of peace.
People waited, bound by cloying doubts.
Their leaders had departed. Now, alone,
They heard the steps of tyranny approach.

In London's Piccadilly, on a stand,
Where sports results were often on display,
The vendor had chalked up the French defeat.
'Great Britain in the final', it went on.

In similar vein was Churchill's broadcast speech:
'The news from France is now extremely bad,
And for her gallant people we all grieve.
Nothing will change our feelings for the French,
Or stem our faith in France's genius.
But what has happened alters not our task.
For we alone are champions in arms,
Defending now the cause of all the world.
To earn this honour we shall do our best.
We shall defend this island, and shall fight,
Invincible beside our Empire kin,
Till Hitler's curse is lifted from mankind.
For I am sure that all will come aright.'

12 Tragedy at Mers-el-Kebir
Summer 1940

With France defeated, and the present threat
Of German landings from the sea and air,
The House of Commons needed once again
To hear from Churchill how the country stood.
His speech was on the day of Waterloo,
But he did not remind the French of this,
Nor dwell upon their new catastrophe.

The members listened, heartened by his words
Of rising modulation, emphasis
And frequent pauses, carefully prolonged:
'In this great crisis let each man reflect,
And search his conscience. All are culpable.
The future, not the past, is our concern.
Our battle-hardened troops, our finest men,
Are now within this island. What is more,
Dominion forces and our new Home Guard
Stand with them; and the Navy – don't forget
That on the sea we have superior power,
By much more now than in the former war.
Meanwhile there may be raids by parachute,
Or airborne landings. We shall deal with these.
That leaves but one great issue to be faced –
Herr Hitler's air force. Can it be destroyed?
We have already gained the mastery,
In combat over France, and at Dunkirk.
In fighting over England, every plane
That we shoot down is totally a loss,
Whilst our brave pilots and their fine machines
May land on friendly soil and fight again.
On every man and woman all depends.

Whatever our station, let us not forget
These famous lines that once described a king:
"He nothing common did nor mean,
Upon that memorable scene."
I see great cause for work and vigilance,
But none at all for panic or despair.
Our just demands remain. Our friends abroad,
The suffering French, the Czechs, the Poles, the Dutch,
Belgians, Norwegians, all are joined with us.
Our cause is theirs, and all shall be restored.
The battle of France is lost, but ours begins.
Upon this battle everything depends:
This Christian culture, our own British life,
The future of the British Commonwealth.
The might and fury of the German race
Will soon be turned on us; for Hitler knows
That he will have to break our island home,
Or lose the war. If we defeat him,
Europe may be free, and all the world
May then be raised to broad and sunlit lands.
But if we fail, then not ourselves alone,
But every nation, all we know and love,
Will sink in the abyss – a new Dark Age,
Protracted by perverted sciences.
Let us endure and, in a thousand years,
They'll say of Britain and her Commonwealth –
Of British folk – this was their finest hour!'

As one admirer said who'd heard him speak:
'Thank God we have this man at such a time.'
The man himself, as he was wont to do,
Had found an armchair in the smoking-room,
And read the evening paper, quite absorbed,
As if it were the only source of news.

In the evening Churchill spoke again,
Broadcasting to the nation what he'd said

Within the intimate chamber of the House.
But now he sounded tired, and as he read,
He smoked his now ubiquitous cigar.
He did not like to speak with microphones,
Devoid of any audience to see,
Of faces that responded, shouts or laughs,
Of sentiment, emotion, taunts and cheers.
But even so, the people were inspired.

Great Britain stood alone. Her people knew
That soon the Germans might invade these isles.
Their leader's mood reflected their resolve.
Few talked of peace, of granting Hitler terms,
Though Churchill could not totally ignore
What might be offered, even whilst he said
That he himself would never compromise.

What most concerned the government was the fate
Of France's navy since the Armistice.
No foreigners would gain control of it –
So Darlan promised. Who could trust him now,
For did he have the power to keep his word?
The Germans had demanded that the French
Hand over all their fleet. The *Führer* said
It would not be employed by Germany.
The Admiral was an honourable man;
But who had faith in Hitler's promises?

What Churchill had conveyed to Roosevelt –
That with the British navy Axis power
Endangered all the western hemisphere –
Was emphasised by this immediate threat.
The warships of the French – the *Richelieu*,
The *Jean Bart*, *Strasbourg*, *Dunkerque* and *Bretagne*,
And many other boats of every type –
Would quite transform the *Kriegmarine*'s attempt
To land an army on the British shore.

Churchill was certain: at whatever cost,
The Germans must not have this battle fleet.

The Admiralty was told to make a plan
To seize all ships of France in British ports,
To shadow those at sea, and be prepared
To sink the ones in harbours of the French.
Of all his grave decisions, Churchill said,
This one he hated most. What could be worse
Than turning on an ally and a friend?
It was unnatural. Yet it would be done.
His message to the Admiral in command
Revealed his own distaste for this cruel act:
'No Admiral has been faced with such a task,
So difficult and disagreeable;
But we have total confidence in you,
And know you'll act with absolute resolve.'

Upon the French themselves the choice would fall.
A list of options would be offered them:
To join Britain against the common foe;
To sail to British ports with skeleton crews;
To decommission boats in neutral ports;
Or, finally, to sink them where they were.
Were none of these to be acceptable,
The British navy would ensure by force
That no French warships reached the enemy.

In British harbours many ships were seized.
At Alexandria the French complied,
Discharging oil and neutralising guns.
At Casablanca *Jean Bart* was entrapped;
And *Richelieu*, the strongest ship afloat,
Was damaged by the British at Dakar.
Yet at Mers-el-Kebir a dreadful scene
Unfolded like an ancient tragedy.

The French commander, Admiral Gensoul,
Received Vice-Admiral Somerville's request
To choose an option, whilst the British ships
Patrolled beyond the port with loaded guns.
There was a long delay. Gensoul had asked
For orders from his own superiors
In Petain's government. They would not relent.
They sent a further force to strengthen him,
Which British decrypts showed was on the way.
Meanwhile Gensoul was trapped. Magnetic mines
Had now been laid across the harbour mouth.

In London, Churchill shuffled to and fro,
Muttering how terrible it was.
Someone told him Somerville's demands
Had not included decommissioning.
'To add that now will let the French assume
That we are weakening', were his only words.

At last a final message was despatched.
'If, by dusk, the French have not complied,
You must then sink them.' But it was received
When all was over. British guns had sunk
The battleship *Bretagne*. *Provence* was beached.
The *Dunkerque* ran aground; and naval planes,
Launched from the British carrier, *Ark Royal*,
Completed the bombardment from the air.
Only the *Strasbourg*, braving mines and guns,
Escaped from port, to safety at Toulon.
Twelve hundred former comrades had been killed.

It fell to Churchill then to tell the House
Of why and how this ruthless act was done.
He spoke for thirty minutes. When he stopped,
The whole House rose and cheered, quite unrestrained.
He sat surprised and moved; his face grew pink,
And tears rolled down his cheeks. For most had feared –

As he had done – the risk, of letting Hitler
Seize the fleet of France. And now they knew
They had a leader fearless to pursue
The path of victory; even to accept
The wrath of former allies, and the pain.

Around the world this devastating act
Removed all doubts of Britain's real intent.
Opinion in America was changed.
Mers-el-Kebir convinced the President
That, come what may, the British would fight on.

As for the French, they hated what was done;
But Charles de Gaulle, though grieved, was statesmanlike.
On his escape he had been well received,
And given help to represent those French
Who had not joined Petain's new regime.
Now when he broadcast to his countrymen,
His words displayed a splendid dignity:
'In every Frenchman, from our very depths,
Comes pain and anger at this tragedy.
But, at some time, our common enemy
Would have employed our ships for his own ends.
It is far better that they were destroyed.
We French must realise that, if England lose,
Our bondage is confirmed. We stand as one,
Our great and ancient nations, win or lose.'

13 The Threat of Invasion
Summer 1940

Only the narrow seas now stood between
The might of German arms and Britain's fate.
The western coast of Europe – all its ports
From Norway's fjords to the Pyrenees –
Was occupied by forces of the Reich.
Even the ocean seaways, whence there came
From Empire sources and America
The vital succour of both men and goods,
Were threatened now by German submarines
And surface raiders from Atlantic ports.
The map of Europe, darkened by the stain
Of Nazi power from Poland to the west,
Gave evidence enough of Britain's plight.
Her island people now stood quite alone,
Whilst Germany, itself more populous,
Abetted by the Fascist Pact of Steel,
Controlled, by force of arms, so many lands,
Their populations, industries and arms.
And, to the east, the Russians acquiesced
In Adolf Hitler's crude rapacity.

Yet many people felt a strange relief
That now they were alone; no more involved
In seeing lovers sent to die abroad,
Or sons and brothers, where their fathers lay
Beneath the earth of foreign battlefields;
No more the painful choices to be made
Of how much should be sacrificed for France,
How many precious aircraft to be flown
To alien skies, to leave their wreckage there,

And youthful pilots dead, or prisoners,
Who could be now defending native land.

This was a strange midsummer time of rest,
Amidst the feverish action of a war,
When past and future were but idle dreams,
And brilliant sunshine burnt away all fear.
It was a moment outside passing time,
A place of stillness, like an ancient church
Whose years of prayer had sanctified the stone
And cleansed the air of every sound but one.
Who then could fear the German paratroops,
Or hordes of field-grey soldiers on the shore,
The screaming *Stukas*, crash of masonry,
The siren's call to shelter from the blast,
The hideous gas mask, carried in a box,
And pain of mutilation, or of death?

So work went on to fortify these isles.
Along the Channel coast barbed rolls of wire
Protected beaches, mines were laid at sea,
And gun emplacements stood on cliffs and knolls
To enfilade the barges full of troops.
Churchill himself had ordered mustard gas
To be prepared for use, if landings came,
And burning oil might set the waves aflame.

He visited the coast, and looked across
At Cap Gris-Nez, where German guns now stood.
He hoped to see an air raid. All that came
Were several Spitfires, glinting in the Sun.
At Brighton he discussed defensive plans,
And said that buses should be commandeered.
There, within Royal Albion Hotel,
Beside the empty pier and esplanade,
He met Montgomery, who was in command,
A soldier marked, like him, for destiny.

At dinner Churchill was amazed to find
The general drank no wine and did not smoke;
But they agreed on military needs,
Especially on mobility by bus.

Experience in France confirmed the view,
Which Churchill's earlier studies bred in him,
That in defence reserves must be retained
To send with speed to threatened areas.
He did not want a British general
To say 'Aucune', as Gamelin did in France.
Landings would be impeded on the beach,
But some would still succeed. The test would be
When, further inland, mobile forces came,
Of chosen troops, with tanks and air support.

But even so, as Churchill often said,
The first line of defence was Britain's fleet.
Salt sea will drown them, he was wont to say;
And when the admirals told him they would keep
Their capital ships far out of bombing range,
He said he knew that, once invasion came,
They would not linger far from Dover straits.

A senior civil servant later spoke
Of how the Premier worked throughout this time.
His home and office had no frontiers.
Within his study, bedroom, or his lounge,
He might be working – anywhere at all.
At almost any hour a summons went
To Ministers, officials, or his staff.
Then he'd dictate, correct and re-dictate.
Orders might be given as one sat
Within the family circle, or at meals.
A member of his personal entourage,
On being asked to see him in his room,
Found him in bed, dictating to a scribe,
Beside a box half full of documents.

In dressing gown of red, and with cigar,
He gazed at his black cat from time to time,
Which sprawled upon the bed, and said to it,
With much affection, 'Nelson, darling cat'.

After the armistice, signed at Compiegne,
The German *Führer* made a Paris tour.
He saw the Opera, and La Madeleine,
Drove up the Champs Elysees, briefly stopped
At Arc de Triomphe and the Eiffel Tower,
And stood in silence at Les Invalides,
Before the marble tomb of Bonaparte.
By evening he'd returned to take command
Within his field headquarters. He remarked
To Albert Speer, his favourite architect,
That, when they'd finished building in Berlin,
Paris would be a shadow. Then he spoke,
At that same place where seven years before
The Reichstag had confirmed his tyranny,
To all the Nazi leaders and the men
Who'd won the famous victory over France –
Goering, Brauchitsch, Halder and the rest –
Though Hitler believed that they had made mistakes,
That his own judgment had secured the prize.

That day he was the conqueror, and showed
An overwhelming confidence and pride,
Yet mixed with some humility for those,
The mass of German people, who admired
His plebeian birth and populist appeal.
His style, this day, was not hysterical.
The gestures with his hands, his swaying form,
The gentler modulation of his voice,
Were all attuned to show him as a man
Intent on reason, not on brutal war.
He dwelt upon the *Wehrmacht*'s victory,
The achievements of the generals, of the role

Of Hermann Goering, elevated now
To Marshal of the Reich, above the rank
Of all but Hitler. Then he emphasised
The strong position Germany now held,
And made an offer to his enemy:
'I feel it is my duty in this hour,
Before my conscience, to make one appeal,
To reason and to common sense abroad.
To Britain I appeal, not as a foe
Defeated, begging favours, but as one
Who speaks, in victory, yet in reason's name.
I do not see why this war should go on.
I grieve to think of victims it will take.
In England Mr. Churchill may object.
Warmongering has always been his work.
No doubt he'll say I'm moved by fear and doubt.
If that is what he says, my way is clear.
My conscience is relieved of what's to come.'

On this occasion – perhaps the only time –
War fever gripped the Berlin populace.
Along the *Führer*'s route were strewn flowers.
To frenzied cries the masses raised their arms
In Nazi salutation. Workers pressed
To leave their factory jobs, and to enlist.
Wilhelm Keitel, Chief of High Command,
Known as the lackey – 'Lakeitel' –
Described the *Führer* as a great warlord:
'The greatest of all time', 'Lakeitel' said.
Incessant propaganda fed the hate
That people felt for Britain, which alone
Now stood frustrating German victory.
They thirsted to destroy this enemy,
Their old opponent, ever at their throat.

The offer Hitler made gave no good grounds
For those in Britain seeking compromise.

Most were agreed to treat it with contempt.
The British press dismissed it. Few could think
It gave the slightest prospect of a peace
Where Europe would be free, or Britain left,
With honour, as an independent State.

Meanwhile, in England, Churchill spent some days
At home at Chartwell in the Weald of Kent.
Wartime had left the gardens rather wild,
But still he fed his goldfish in the ponds,
The birds, the old swan on the lake,
And shouted at his 'darling' family cat.

Between these gentle pastimes, in his mind
The war reserved its place, and plans were made.
He thought of armoured groups and 'panther springs'
To raid the enemy coast and then depart;
Of British bombers over Germany,
In growing strength, till even if 'that man'
Should reach the Caspian Sea, he would return
To find a fire ablaze in his backyard;
Of how to use brass bands to raise morale;
Of British soldiers' preference for beef.
But always Churchill thought of Britain's plight:
Invasion threats, the vigilance required.
'Take one with you', was a new motif
To sharpen people's appetite for war.

He still found time for personal sympathy.
A brilliant young commander, who'd been killed,
A pioneer of submarine patrols,
Was praised by Churchill for his famous deeds.
He wrote by hand to comfort the bereaved.
In her reply, the sailor's mother said:
'We long have believed you are the only one
Who can bring England out of these dark times.'

Despite the danger, Britain still was calm.
There was no panic; order was maintained.
Occasionally a false alarm was heard,
When church bells rang to indicate attack.
But then new rules were made –for greater proof
Of German paratroops, or other scares.
Once it had been reported that they'd come
Disguised as nuns and travelling by bus!

In fact, the enemy had not evolved
Coherent plans to land within these shores.
For 'Sea Lion' was a hasty compromise
Between the service chiefs of Hitler's Reich.
The navy, under Raeder, feared the risks
Of meeting a superior naval power,
And wanted to defend a narrow path
Across the Channel. But the army chiefs
Demanded landings on a broader front,
From Folkstone to the Solent. All they'd met
Were river crossings on the continent.
Amphibious action was quite alien
To Prussian generals schooled on Clausewitz.
In Norway, under cover of surprise,
They'd quickly seized the ill-defended ports;
Whereas in England forces would dispute
Each yard of beach or dock or hinterland.
As General Jodl later was to say
The German plans to invade the British Isles
Were much like those of Caesar. It was left
To Marshal Goering and his *Luftwaffe*
To make conditions ripe for an assault.

Whoever could control the skies above
Might dominate the narrow waterway;
And air power would be crucial for the troops
Engaged upon the beaches. Goering, though,
As always over-confident and brash,

Assured the *Führer* that he would defeat
The British air force in a few short weeks,
And bomb the navy's ports. Indeed, he thought
That Britain might be made to sue for peace
Without the *Wehrmacht* playing any part.
Hitler allowed himself to be convinced.
He came from middle Europe. English seas
Were not within his landsman's *Weltanschauung*.
Jodl and Raeder welcomed Goering's hopes,
And quietly shelved their joint invasion plans.

14 The Battle of Britain
Summer 1940

Hitler was baffled. Why did England choose
To fight a war that she had clearly lost?
He did not know the English. He had seen
The men of Munich, eager to comply,
Incompetence in Norway, and in France
A brief endeavour, followed by retreat.
He did not know their innate stubbornness,
Their independence, how when they were roused
They could be ruthless. Neither had he learnt
How, with the change in English leadership,
There was a change of heart; how Churchill now
Was truly but a representative,
The spokesman of their readiness to fight.

The *Luftwaffe* could fly from aerodromes
From Norway to the Cape of Finisterre.
Attacks would come from many compass points,
At any time, to targets unforeseen.
All now would turn on how the battle fared
Above the south-east counties and the sea.
But first they chose the naval ports and ships
To give support to Admiral Raeder's plans;
Though Goering hoped the British would respond
By fighting in the air. He was not wrong.
From forward bases British aircraft flew
To meet the attackers high above the sea.
Whereas the *Stuka* bombers' screaming dives
Had terrorised the armies of the French,
They were no match for British fighter planes.

Yet Marshal Goering entertained no doubts.
His *Luftwaffe*, victorious in France,
Would soon destroy the British fighter force,
And then his heavier bombers would be free
To shatter English cities, till the time
When Hitler could dictate his terms of peace.

Goering's opponent in the R.A.F.
Was Air Chief Marshal Dowding, who'd refused
To send more fighters to the war in France,
And thus deplete the British air defence.
Unlike the flamboyant Goering, he was quiet,
Teetotal, Christian, and intransigent.
He'd flown, like Goering, in the former war,
And, scheduled to retire, retained command,
With Churchill's backing, at this crucial hour.

Dowding had said, before the war began,
That , for this country, far the best defence
Was fear of fighters; that potential foes
Should know they faced a powerful fighter force.
'I must record my view', the Marshal wrote,
'That home defence command should not be seen
As equal with the rest, but have first claim,
Since on this would depend the very life
Of Britain as a nation.' For this end
He'd argued unashamedly with those –
The bomber force commanders, army men
Who wanted fighter cover on the ground,
And politicians at the Treasury –
Who'd sought to limit his supply of planes.
This 'Dowding Doctrine' Churchill had approved,
Despite the pressure he himself had felt,
When France was failing, and her desperate cries
Had driven him to make some compromise.

The time had come when all was justified.
On Dowding's pilots and their fine machines –

The Hurricane and Spitfire monoplanes,
Designed for manoeuvrability and speed –
Survival of the nation would depend.
Dowding, too, had overseen the work
Of building up an integrated scheme
Of radar stations and the ground control
Which organised the squadrons in the air.
Ultra decrypts warned of new attacks,
And radio kept pilots well informed.
All this was due to Dowding. Churchill knew
What this man had achieved. So he it was
Who'd overruled demands that he retire.
He knew his judgment, long experience,
His patriotism and his sturdy will.
So intuition told him to retain
This fighting airman for the crucial task.

Soon wave on wave of German bombers came –
The square-tipped *Heinkels*, slender *Dorniers* –
To Manston, Hawkinge, Lympne, Biggin Hill,
To crater runways, blow up grounded planes,
And damage vital centres of control;
Whilst on the industrial cities, those that made
The aircraft frames and engines, bombs now fell
To cut supplies of precious fighter planes.

It was a warm, bright Summer. People watched
In market towns and villages of Kent,
As, high above, the aircraft left their trails
Of harmless vapour, or black shrouds of smoke.

Churchill could do little. He had warned
That this air battle would be critical.
Now he must wait, and like the crowds in Kent,
Watch helplessly below, whilst others fought.
Doubtless he recalled how years before
He'd almost learnt to fly, in crude machines,

And narrowly escaped an accident;
How Clementine, then pregnant, had appealed
Against his rashness; how he had foreseen
The crucial future role of air defence,
And fought in Parliament for greater strength
To match the *Luftwaffe*'s development.

Often now he visited a room
Where fighter operations were controlled,
And looked with rapt attention at the map
That showed the opposing forces in the air.
He could not intervene, but only trust
The quiet efficient staff, who marked with care
The planes of either side, those in reserve,
In transit to engage the enemy,
Or held transfixed in duels of sudden death.

On leaving, once, he turned towards his aide,
And said in tones unusually subdued:
'Don't speak to me; I've never been so moved.'
He thought how few these British pilots were;
Not like the massive armies he had seen
At Omdurman, or on the western front.
'The fewer men, the greater share of honour.
God's will! I pray thee, wish not one man more.'

These words of Shakespeare echoed in his mind,
When later he addressed the Lower House.
'The gratitude of every home', he said,
'In Britain, in the Empire, in the world,
Except in the abodes of guilty men,
Goes out to British airmen, those who fight
Undaunted by the odds, by mortal threats,
And, by devotion, turn the tide of war.
Never in the field of human conflict
Was so much owed by many to so few.'
Throughout the nation Churchill's speech aroused

A deep respect for those he had so praised.
But, in the R.A.F., the latter words
Referred, they said, to mess bills in arrears.

Although the battle occupied his mind,
He had to deal with other urgent tasks.
Bomber Command had suffered heavy loss;
Reconnaissance of continental ports
Showed German barges ready to invade;
Italian forces threatened to attack
Across the Egyptian border. All required
Intelligent decisions, even whilst
The fate of Britain hung in Summer skies.

Tactics had changed. The British Hurricanes
Were now directed at the bomber force,
Whilst roving Spitfires fought the *Messerschmitts*,
Who flew in closer escort high above.
Every day to Churchill's notice came
The toll of aircraft lost, the new reserves,
The pilots killed or rescued on each side.
No one knew just how the Germans fared,
But British airfields were in desperate straits.
The vital radar stations were intact,
But pilots were exhausted, fighting now
On last extremities, of body, will,
And, in the final test, of self-respect.

On ground crews, too, the strain was now intense.
Midst constant bombing, they prepared the planes:
Refuelling, arming, testing radios,
Checking engines, replacing oxygen.
A breaking point would come, when able men,
And aircraft fit to fly, would be too few
To stop the onslaught from the eastern sky.

But now a twist of fate, or Providence,
Directed that the battle should be fought

With new objectives. London had been bombed –
Most probably in error or by chance –
And, in retaliation, Churchill sent
A force of heavy bombers to Berlin,
Where Goering vowed no British bombs would fall.
The *Führer* was incensed; he swore revenge
To massive crowds in Berlin's *Sportpalast*.
The *Luftwaffe* would wipe out Britain's towns.
For had not Hermann Goering reaffirmed
The British would surrender to the threat
Of mass destruction of her urban life,
As Holland did when Rotterdam was struck?
He did not know, in his splenetic rage,
That he had saved their fighter aerodromes.

The Londoners were not dismayed by war,
That touched them in their homes and city streets.
The wailing sirens sent them quietly down
To camp on station platforms overnight,
Where some brought carpets, furniture and beds,
And put up flags, or portraits of the King.

What people called 'invasion weekend' came,
When tides and phase of moon were favourable,
And all along the southern coast lay troops,
In fields and farmyards, ordered now to sleep
In readiness for battle. Churchill, too,
Had practised firing on a rifle range,
With some success – though smoking a cigar.

Daylight attacks on London had not ceased,
Despite the heavy loss of German planes.
So Churchill went to witness once again
The conduct of a battle in the air,
Which might, this time, encourage or repel
The imminent invasion from the sea.

Within the bomb-proof operations room,
Below the ground at Uxbridge, Churchill met
The tall New Zealander, Vice-Marshal Park,
Who'd been severely wounded on the Somme,
But then became a pilot. Now he gave
The battle orders to the fighter force,
For he controlled the conflict hour to hour,
Whilst Dowding was in charge from day to day.
Park's Group 11 was the chief defence
Of south-east England. He decided how
His fighters intercepted every raid,
Whilst keeping back reserves, until he knew
Which target was most heavily attacked.

Churchill was invited, with his wife,
To sit above the plotters' large-scale map.
In grey-blue uniform, young personnel,
Both men and women, sat below, alert,
Attended closely by telephonists.
Electric bulbs, in columns on the wall,
Denoted the location of the planes.
The lighted ones showed squadrons 'standing by',
Others at readiness, or in the air –
Those which had seen a coming bomber force,
And those in action (signified in red),
And finally those now returning home.

Some officers sat weighing up reports
From Observation Corps across the land,
Who were the eyes within the radar screen
That monitored the bombers out at sea
As they approached the Kent and Sussex coast.
Another group, of army officers,
Controlled the anti-aircraft batteries.

'At present all is quiet', said Marshal Park;
But, fifteen minutes later, work began

On plotting planes across the table map.
Forty plus were coming from Dieppe.
The wall display began to glow with light.
Squadrons were on stand-by. Signals came
Of larger groups of bombers – sixty plus,
Then sixty more, and eighty; every wave
Of Germans aircraft marked by pushing discs
Along the several lines of their approach.

The bulbs began to show the fighters rise,
The Hurricanes and Spitfires, leaving still
Some half a dozen squadrons on the ground.
They had to climb above the enemy,
Engage them briefly, and return again
For fuel and ammunition. German planes
Might bomb the airfields, so the air control
Was charged with keeping fighters overhead.

The red bulbs glowed. Most squadrons were engaged.
As messages came through, the plotters moved
Across the busy map the nameless discs
That represented friend and foe alike.
Behind the Churchills, walking back and forth,
With vigilant eyes on each development,
The Air Vice-Marshal gave his broad commands,
Whilst others worked the detailed orders out
To send to fighter stations: cover raids,
Withdraw some planes from battle, call reserves,
Or reinforce the areas at threat.

Churchill sat in silence, quite absorbed,
His head bent down upon the scene below,
A new cigar unlit. At each red light,
He frowned aggressively; whilst Clementine,
Less passionately engaged, turned frequently
To watch him. This, he knew, was England's war,
Fought over native land, no more in France,

By Englishmen, and those of like intent,
Men from the Empire, gallant Poles and Czechs.

All squadrons now were airborne. Bulbs went off
To indicate no planes in readiness.
And now, amongst the discs for *Luftwaffe*,
Were some that showed high-flying *Messerschmitts*.
Park spoke to Dowding on the telephone.
Immediately, from an adjacent Group,
Three squadrons more were sent, in case a raid
Should catch 11 Group as they rearmed.
The aerodromes, and London, were at risk.

Yet all was calm, and officers still spoke
In steady, almost casual, monotones,
As though the board of discs was but a game,
A battleground of model aeroplanes,
Not marking real machines and mortal men.
But Park, in fact, was anxious. He stood still,
Behind the chair of his subordinate.

Churchill enquired, 'Now what are our reserves?'
'There are none', Park replied. In Churchill's mind
Another scene, so different in its form,
Was conjured up – of Paris, Quai d'Orsay,
Where Frenchmen once had sat, with mournful looks,
Aware of their defeat, as Gamelin spoke.
He saw again the splendid gilded room,
The smoke of bonfires on the lawn outside
Of archives burnt by Foreign Office staff.
'Where are the French reserves?' Churchill had asked.
'*Aucune*', Gamelin had said. There was no hope.
Was that same tragedy to be replayed?
This time the R.A.F. without reserves;
This time a war of movement in the air,
Just as the German tanks had fought in France,
Exploiting points of weakness, cutting through

Inadequate defences, breaking down
The last resistant forces, till the hour
When all was shattered, armies, aircraft, men?

He turned aside from such imaginings.
He was no fatalist; events were made
By actions, battles won by what men did,
By those brave pilots someone had described
As blonde young men, blue-eyed, with ruddy cheeks,
Who looked as though they ought to be at school.
How few indeed they were! To Park's reply
Churchill said nothing, but he looked most grave.
Yet Clementine was smiling. Had she heard
What Marshal Park had said? He did not know.
He grunted at her, incoherently.

Upon the map below the discs had moved.
Most squadrons had descended to refuel.
They lacked protection. But the plotters showed
An eastward movement of the German planes.
There were no new attacks. Above the room,
The warning sirens sounded the 'all clear'.
Vice-Marshal Park was grateful they had come.
'Today we have been strained beyond our means,
But still we have repelled them', he remarked.

That evening Churchill heard the day's report
Of many ships torpedoed, other news,
Of losses, direful warnings, bad delays,
But, last of all, his secretary said,
'All is redeemed by victory in the air.'

Indeed that day was perhaps the turning point.
The *Luftwaffe* had been prepared for war
Above the *Wehrmacht*, trained to give support,
A vital arm of Blitzkrieg, as they'd proved
In battles over Poland and in France.

Their aeroplanes had never been designed
For this strategic warfare, for long flights
With heavy bomb-loads, and the constant need
For fighter escorts over sea and land.
Their Me109s had not the range
To fly beyond the English capital,
And little fuel for dogfights over Kent.
They'd fought as bravely as the R.A.F.,
But they had been defeated. Now, at last,
The world had seen the ending of the myth
That Adolf Hitler was invincible.

Two days later 'Sealion' was postponed.
An *Ultra* decrypt brought the welcome news.
The chief deterrent, said the German Staff,
Was large scale action by the British fleet.
What had 'the few' achieved? There was no doubt.
With air control the Germans might have risked
A sea invasion, or as Goering said,
They might have forced the British to their knees
By aerial bombardment. Churchill knew
What debt was owed to that courageous band
Who'd fought in Britain's skies so gallantly.

15 The Blitz
Autumn 1940

'We'll raze the British cities to the ground.'
Thus spake the *Führer*, in his bitter rage.
The aerodromes were saved, but in return
The price was paid by unarmed citizens.
A heavy daylight raid had been repulsed
By British fighters. Night would now conceal
The droning bombers, pregnant with their loads.
What could protect the Londoners by night?
No more could fighter pilots hunt their prey
In sunlit skies or silver-ribboned clouds.
But now, beyond the fearful whistling noise
Of falling bombs, explosions, crackling fires,
Came suddenly, one evening, deeper roars
Of anti-aircraft guns, whose deafening bursts
Did much to raise morale – however slight
Their impact on the enemy unseen.
Now narrow cones of searchlights pierced the sky
And briefly lit a cross-marked fuselage.
Night-fighters prowled through darkness. Tracer lit,
For fleeting seconds, scores of blackened wings.

Beneath the aircraft – havoc. In the docks
Incendiaries raised myriads of fires,
Of wood and rubber, sugar, tar and oil,
Grains and other foodstuffs, paint and gas.
The molten tar obstructed rescue work,
And sulphurous clouds of smoke made rumours spread
That German planes were dropping mustard gas.
From burning factories swarms of rats appeared.
As mooring ropes caught fire, the smouldering craft
Were soon adrift upon the shining Thames.

On moonlit nights the German pilots saw
The wharves and houses well-defined below.
Always the snaking river showed the way,
And then the fires, whose ruddy glow was seen
By shocked observers on the Sussex Downs.

East Enders' homes were burning. Families fled
To brick-built shelters, schools or underground,
In basements or in cellars, where they slept,
Or waited open-eyed to hear the sound
Of 'all-clear' sirens. Soon the bombing spread,
To central London, to the West End shops,
To Buckingham Palace and to Downing Street.

The King and Queen were shaken by a bomb
Within the courtyard, thirty yards away.
Whilst, after Churchill told domestic staff
To move to shelters under Downing Street,
A bomb destroyed the kitchen. He himself
Would often climb to have a rooftop view,
Where, unconcerned, he'd watch the bursting shells,
The dotted lines of tracer and the glow
Of many fires in the proximity.
One night he quoted to his startled guests,
Who'd been invited to this lofty scene,
A verse, most apposite, of Tennyson:

> Hear the heavens fill with shouting,
>   and there rain'd a ghastly dew
> From the nations' airy navies
>   grappling in the central blue.

He visited the stricken Londoners,
When fires still raged, and ruined buildings stood
Like skeletons amidst the rubble heaps;
Where tiny paper flags –the Union Jack –
Waved bravely on some workers' shattered homes.
A crowd of people, mainly very poor,
Had gathered where a shelter was destroyed,

And forty had been killed. When Churchill came,
Unsure of his reception, he was mobbed.
'Good old Winnie!' many of them cried.
'We can take it. Give it to 'em back!'
A woman shouted, 'See he really cares.'
She'd seen that he could not restrain his tears.

Luftwaffe concentration on the docks
Meant East End families suffered most of all.
As death tolls rose, with many others maimed,
Some grew resentful that they bore the brunt,
These manual workers in their meagre homes,
Which were most vulnerable to blast and fire.
'If this goes on', one close observer said,
'There will be revolution.' Churchill thought
Of when, so long before, he had attacked
The bastions of landed privilege,
And, as a Liberal, coveted support
From all who worked by hand or heart or brain.
His father's creed still animated him:
To trust the people. But he did not claim
To represent the workers and their cause.
He fiercely had opposed the general strike,
And had no truck with Socialism's aims.

But now he was their leader. Few could doubt
That he alone might save them from this plight.
They recognised his courage in themselves.
His slow, deliberate voice, those Summer days,
Heard in their parlours, or their sitting rooms,
Awoke in them a long-forgotten sense
Of fellowship with others, of one land,
Of undivided people, of one aim,
Which might be labelled 'victory', but which touched
On something deeper, near perhaps to love.
There was no revolution. They all knew
The rich lay dead in rubble, just the same.

Swimming baths were often mortuaries,
Where corpses lay discreetly covered up,
And grim-faced men, with bags for body parts,
Attempted to identify the dead.
Schools and churches were assembly points,
Though some were hit before the buses came
To take to safety women and the old,
And children lost or orphaned. None could tell
How long it would continue. Churchill said –
But only to his colleagues, not elsewhere –
'That as destruction grows, the less is done,
Since bombs will fall on ruined areas.'
But how long could the Londoners endure?

Amidst the blitz what he especially saw
Was courage, resolution and the will
To carry on the war with Germany.
But Clementine observed much more besides.
She saw the air-raid shelters of the poor,
And noted down their grave deficiencies –
Of space, and bedding, sanitation, warmth,
Facilities for children and the old.
She was outspoken; Ministers were blamed,
And Churchill, too, was often importuned.

His broadcast speech diffused both pride and hope:
'Our famous island race, Herr Hitler thinks,
Can be destroyed by slaughter from the air.
But what he's doing kindles in our hearts,
And in the British people everywhere,
A fire whose embers will not cease to glow
When London's conflagration has expired,
A fire to burn with strong, consuming flames,
Till every vestige of his tyranny
Has been burnt out of Europe; till the world –
The Old World and the New – can join hands
To rebuild once again the sacred homes

Where liberty and honour may still live.
We all stand together, holding firm.
How much we can admire those services,
Especially London's gallant Fire Brigade,
Whose work has been so long and dangerous.
The whole free world is marvelling at the strength,
The fortitude, of London's citizens,
The end of whose ordeal we cannot see.
Our fighting forces know they leave behind
A people who will never flinch nor fail,
However hard the struggle may become.
Out of the heart of suffering we draw
The very means of hope. We shall survive;
And win a victory not for us alone,
Bur for mankind and better days to come.'

About this time a journalist had said
That Churchill was not born an orator.
When he was asked, Churchill himself agreed.
'Not born, not in the least', he had replied.
'It's been hard work', and evidence confirmed
This modest view of his accomplishment.
For Churchill often wrote a speech in full,
Dictating some, or others by his hand,
Inserting or deleting frequently,
And then might mark the first word of each line
To guide him when he spoke. Lord Birkenhead,
A Parliamentary friend, once said of him,
That he had spent the best years of his life
In preparation of impromptu speech.

Meanwhile invasion barges filled the ports
Along the hostile coast, where German troops
Still practised for an imminent attack.
They knew no more than British soldiers did
Of Hitler's real intentions. He had seen
The *Luftwaffe* repulsed, and heard the doubts

Of Admiral Raeder and the *Kriegsmarine*.
His thoughts were turned on Russia. Was she not
The only hope of Churchill, all that stood
Between the Reich and total victory?
He briefed his generals to prepare a plan
To smash the Russian army, which – he believed –
Was weakened by the Tukhachevsky purge,
And proved defective in the Finnish war.

Churchill knew that 'Sealion' was postponed.
He guessed it was unlikely till the Spring,
But publicly he called for vigilance.
Everything depended on morale.
Were Goering's terror bombing to succeed,
Invasion barges would not be required.

Not only East End workers, M.P.s, too,
Now called for Britain to retaliate
By bombing German cities. Churchill met
A group of them within the Commons' bar,
Where he would sit and read the *Evening News*.
He told them he believed the R.A.F.
Should choose strategic targets, not revenge.
But he himself gave orders that land mines –
Which German planes had dropped by parachute,
With terrible effect in urban streets –
Should likewise be deployed on German towns.

The *Luftwaffe* changed its targets once again.
London had not surrendered, so they turned
On Britain's provincial cities, often those
That manufactured armaments and planes.
Four hundred people died in Coventry,
Where, too, the old cathedral was destroyed.
Birmingham, Bristol, Liverpool and Leeds,
And many other cities suffered raids.

Churchill found time, amidst his many cares,
To visit ruined areas and meet
The hardy men and women who'd survived.
He could not offer much, but he was now
The symbol of their own resilience.
His squat, pugnacious figure, slightly stooped,
With high black hat, cigar and overcoat,
Striding ahead of others half his age
Across the rubble heaps of dust and brick,
Or leaning, pensive, on his walking stick,
Created where he went a certainty
That he would not be beaten; they were sure.

At lunch one day in London, as he sat
In siren-suit, with whiskey and cigar,
He said he thought this was the kind of war
That suited English people well enough,
When they were used to it. They all preferred
To take part in the battle, at the front,
Rather than looking on, quite helplessly,
At slaughter on the scale of Passchendaele.

No longer did the German bombers fly
By daylight over Britain. They had met
Too fierce a welcome from the R.A.F.
But night-time raids became more accurate,
When German science made a wireless beam
That planes could follow to their target zones.
Churchill and the Cabinet were concerned.
Night fighters could not see the enemy;
And anti-aircraft guns could not protect
So many towns and cities. So he called
On scientists and air force officers,
Who met him to confer at Downing Street.

Many were incredulous, and said
That British aircraft always found their way,

So navigation did not need a beam,
And questioned its existence. Help was sought;
From Dr. Jones, a youthful scientist,
Who could report on detailed evidence.
When the doctor heard the call to go,
He thought, at first, it was a colleague's joke.
But Churchill let him freely speak his mind,
Despite the doubts of his superiors.

He was convincing. Churchill asked him how
The beam could be negated. He was told
How false cross-beams could fool the German planes,
Or jamming could eliminate their beams.
He ordered instant action. 'All I get,'
He angrily declaimed, 'from Air Force Staff,
Is files and files and files.' So Dr Jones
Became, henceforth, a favoured scientist.

Meanwhile Neville Chamberlain had died.
What harsh words Churchill once had used of him,
When Chamberlain, in triumph, had returned
From granting Hitler Czech Sudetenland!
Yet latterly he'd served with diligence
In Churchill's Cabinet. It was his support
That, after France had fallen, gave the lie
To thoughts of peace with Hitler. In Church House –
To which the House of Commons had repaired
For greater safety – Churchill spoke of him.

'The flickering lamp of history stumbles on,
Reviving echoes, memories of the past.
What are they worth, pale gleams of former days?
The only guide is conscience. That alone,
Sincerity in actions, rectitude,
Can shield a man from memory of the past,
From failure of his hopes, from plans upset.
But with this shield, however fates may play,

We march in ranks of honour faultlessly.
It fell to Neville Chamberlain to see,
In times of crisis rarely paralleled,
The disappointment of his cherished hopes.
He was deceived and cheated by a man
Of unexampled wickedness; and yet,
What was his faith that was so much abused?
It was a love of peace, pursuit of peace,
A noble instinct of the human heart,
To strive for peace, however perilous.
Whatever history says of these hard times,
We can be sure of Neville Chamberlain,
That to the utmost of his strength and will,
He sought to save the world from what we face,
This awful war in which we are engaged.
What now do Hitler's frantic gestures mean;
That he, the German *Führer*, looks for peace?
What do his ravings count for, set beside
The silent tomb of Neville Chamberlain?'

16 Dakar
Autumn 1940

The invasion threat had weakened, but at sea
The British navy scarcely could maintain
Sufficient ships to guard the eastern shores,
Whilst still protecting convoys from the west
That brought supplies of food and precious arms.

At last came some relief. For Roosevelt,
Whom Churchill had entreated many times
For fifty old destroyers, found a way
To satisfy the doubts of Congressmen.
Now, in return, America would lease
The bases they required for their defence
In Commonwealth possessions. These old ships
Would fill the dangerous gap, till British yards
Could build her own requirements on the sea.

Amidst invasion scares and London's blitz,
This was but one of many new concerns.
In Egypt General Wavell's army stood
Against Italians many times as great.
Defence of Egypt was most critical
For Britain's Empire. Suez was the key
To India and Australasia,
And in the Middle East lay vital oil,
For Britain, or for Hitler's war machine.

Despite the home front's needs, the choice was made
To send to Egypt half of Britain's tanks.
How could they get there? Admiral Pound was sure
The long route round the Cape alone was safe.
Churchill opposed him. Surely they should make

The passage through Gibraltar to the east,
And run the gauntlet of Italian ships,
And even of their aircraft, for the sake
Of reinforcing Wavell with due speed?
The Chiefs of Staff were adamant. To them,
With wise restraint, the Premier deferred.
Though often he would argue forcibly,
And win them over to his point of view,
He never overruled them, if they stood
United in professional expertise.
In this case they were right. For great delay
Attended Marshal Graziani's force.
Yet, later, Churchill's bolder view prevailed,
When reinforcements took the shorter route.

Other matters could not be ignored:
Ammunition was in short supply
From German bombing of the factories;
Aircraft output was still critical,
Though Churchill praised the work of Beaverbrook,
Who oversaw production of new planes;
The War Office objected to the plan,
Which Churchill had endorsed, for new elites,
Commando units, like the *Wehrmacht* troops
Who'd stormed Eban Emael to such effect.

Further afield, the prospect now arose
Of French possessions in West Africa
Defecting from the Vichy government,
And turning to de Gaulle. Churchill was keen
To give support to such an enterprise
By Free French soldiers. Dakar was the goal.

At Downing Street, de Gaulle and Churchill met.
Within the Cabinet room the table bore
Some coloured maps of western Africa,
And, indicating them from time to time,

The British Premier paced about the room,
Speaking with animation of his plans.
De Gaulle said little, as he heard revealed
How Dakar would soon rally to his cause;
How allied ships would overawe the port,
Whilst Free French envoys, under flags of truce,
Would land to meet the Vichy Governor.
Shots would be fired, for honour's sake alone,
And, by the evening, all would be resolved.
Both sides would drink to common victory.

Though somewhat sceptical, de Gaulle well knew
That his refusal might give Britain cause
To seize Dakar for her own purposes.
In German hands it could become a base
For submarines; and *Richelieu* was there,
An uncompleted major battleship.

A catalogue of mischance intervened.
Free French officers toasted 'à Dakar'
At restaurants in London and elsewhere.
Tricolour leaflets, with the word 'Dakar',
Were scattered accidentally at the Clyde.
From Toulon, Vichy sent a cruiser group
To reinforce the base. By negligence
It was not intercepted at the Straits –
A British Admiral promptly was dismissed –
And reached its destination. At the news
The British Cabinet, and its Chief, agreed
That too much would be lost if conflict grew
Between opposing Frenchmen. Orders went
To cancel action; but a strong reply
From officers commanding at the scene,
Especially from de Gaulle, expressed the will
To fight despite the odds. It was most rare
For Churchill to deter offensive acts
By field commanders eager to engage.

The prize was great. It would be one more step
In wresting French possessions from the grasp
Of Vichy, and those Frenchmen like Laval,
Who would allow the Germans to construct
A U-boat base along the southern route
Of British convoys to the Middle East.
De Gaulle was told to go ahead as planned.

An unaccustomed fog at Dakar's port
Inhibited the Anglo-French approach.
Envoys from de Gaulle were soon rebuffed,
And batteries opened fire on British ships.
It was returned, but then the *Richelieu*,
With guns of fifteen inches, joined the fray.
Some British ships were damaged. News was sent,
Informing London of these hard events.
Churchill replied that, having once begun,
They should continue to the very end.

But greater damage to the British fleet,
And failure of the French to land nearby,
Now threatened grave disaster. All agreed
That action should be halted. Charles de Gaulle,
Determined to succeed, without Dakar,
Instead made landings at the Cameroons,
And from that base he rallied to his side
Free French adherents in West Africa.

The fate of France, a nation much esteemed
By one so versed in European lore,
Was never far from Winston Churchill's mind.
He held the Vichy government in contempt,
But, unlike Charles de Gaulle, reserved the right
To give them credit, if they were inclined
To disregard their German masters' will.
It was still vital for the British cause
That two great ships, the *Richelieu* and *Jean Bart*,

Should not return to Toulon. Darlan's word
Could not alone defend the fleet of France
From falling into Admiral Raeder's hands.

Much would depend on what the people felt.
So Churchill judged the time appropriate
For an appeal by radio to France.
Despite his accent, which his English friends
Found greatly entertaining, Churchill chose
To broadcast in their language to the French.

Michel Saint-Denis gave him some advice,
Which Churchill welcomed, though with some reserve:
'You won't perfect my French; nor should you try.
If it's too good, they'll like me less for that!'
He relished certain words, the Frenchman said,
Like fruit that tasted sweet and succulent.
'Wearing his famous one piece siren suit,
A light blue garment, fastened with a zip,
He sat before me, like a sky blue bear,
Growling at phrases he found hard to say.'

An air raid was in progress high above,
As they descended under Downing Street,
To broadcast from the safety of the rooms
That Churchill called the Annex, far below.
The Frenchman was enthralled by what he saw.
His ears still rang with cannon fire and bombs,
But underground he found a world transformed:
Rooms like a submarine's, with dazzling lights,
The buzz of phones, occasionally a bell,
Typewriters, screens with numbers black or red,
Rubber carpets to absorb the sound,
A small camp bed, like Bonaparte's, he thought.
And finally a table, where there stood,
Beside a bunch of microphones, a team
Of BBC technicians. All was set.
There was an air of quiet efficiency;

Despite the war above, it was serene.
The free world, thought Saint-Denis, has its brain
Within these walls, beneath the London streets.

After an introduction, Churchill spoke:
'*Dieu protege la France*', he proudly said.
'Here in London everyone awaits
Invasion by the armies of the Reich.
So do the fishes. We command the sea,
And soon we shall command the air as well.
Hitler, with the *Duce* by his side,
May soon dismember France. Alsace-Lorraine,
Savoy and Nice, Napoleon's Corsica,
These will be torn away, and more, from France.
I do not mince my words. Not just defeat,
But exploitation, pillage, Hitler seeks.
The language, culture, literature and art,
All that the French have given to the world,
Will be effaced by Nazi gangsterism.
Remember what Napoleon once said:
"These very Prussians who are boastful now,
Were three to one at Jena; even more,
No less than six to one, at Montmirail."
For never will the soul of France be dead.
Do not imagine, as the Germans say,
That we, the English, seek your colonies.
We seek one end alone, and all the time,
To cleanse the world from Nazi pestilence.
You in France, and in your colonies,
May see some useful action to this end.
I will not give more details. Just recall
The words of your Gambetta, when he said
Of France's future, "Think of it always;
But never speak of it." Bright shines the dawn
On all who suffer for the cause of France,
And all the common people in all lands
Who march for truth and justice. *Vive la France!*'

De Gaulle, although disheartened at Dakar,
Had triumphed over failure. Other States –
The Cameroons, Chad and Congo – joined him;
And soon he showed himself, as Churchill wrote,
Much more than just a military man,
By speaking of the Allies' unity.

From Brazzaville his Declaration said:
'Events impose on me this sacred task –
The burden to direct the war for France.
And so I call to war, to sacrifice,
All men and women of the French domain
Who rally to me. Allied with those friends
Whose will is to retrieve the land of France,
Her greatness and her independent power,
Our duty is to hold those territories
Which have declared their loyalty to our cause,
To attack our foes wherever possible,
To mobilise resources, and to keep,
In French possessions, public discipline.'
And finally he said, 'May justice reign!'

He had not told the British of his plans.
The Foreign Office, hoping still to woo
The Vichy government to some compromise,
Were furious at de Gaulle's audacity.
But Churchill knew he was the soul of France;
And that, to Frenchmen, he must never look
As though he were a pawn in English hands.
He needed to be rude to Englishmen.
As Churchill later wrote, in this respect
He showed great perseverance in his task!

The Premier's home at Chequers, which he used
For working weekends, free of London's noise,
Was now considered under threat from bombs.
Instead he used the house of Ditchley Park,

The home of a Conservative M.P.
When Churchill went there, two detectives came
And scoured it from the cellar to the roof,
Then servants with the luggage, and his staff.
A full platoon of soldiers guarded it.
Regular guests were Chiefs of Staff, and those,
Like Brendan Bracken or Lord Beaverbrook,
Who were his most congenial of friends.

17 North African Success
Winter 1940

For Britain to continue in the war
With any hope of winning, aid must come
Across the ocean, from America.
Whilst urgent matters pressed upon his time,
Still Churchill needed frequently to write
To Washington, and Franklin Roosevelt,
With whom he had developed a rapport,
Based on his family background, and the time
That both had spent in naval services.
In correspondence to the President,
He signed himself, not as Prime Minister,
But, mockingly, as 'Former Naval Person'.

There came, at this time, from America
A chief adviser to the President,
One Harry Hopkins, who was soon to be
A confidant of Winston Churchill too.
Slightly built and ailing, Hopkins yet
Possessed great strength of purpose. He ensured
That lend-lease programmes, and the other aid
That Britain so immediately required
Were finally agreed in Washington.
Throughout the war, he would fulfil the role
Of wise and trusted intermediary.
His courage and outspokenness appealed
To Churchill and to Roosevelt alike.
The cause of Britain soon became his own.
On this first visit, he was moved to say,
That on returning to America,
He'd quote his mother's words of long ago:
'Thy people shall be mine. Thy God my God.'

The President himself was keen to help.
He had been re-elected, but required
Support from Congress for the generous plans
He hoped to make for Britain's benefit.
Demands were made for British firms to sell
Their total assets held within the States,
For gold from the Dominions to be claimed,
And even for a U.S. ship to fetch,
Direct from Cape Town, British stocks of gold.

Churchill was firm: 'If need be we will fight
Just with our own resources to the end,
But we alone cannot bring victory.
You might be left to face', his message said,
'A Nazi Europe, allied with Japan,
Whose fleet controlled the oceans of the world,
And whose destructive power would render yours
Unequal to the struggle.' He himself
Could not define the means; all he could say
Was that this was the moment now to act,
To promise Britain what she would require
To fight for their joint interests. 'Find a way,
And we shall save the world from tyranny.'

In response, the President appealed,
Over the heads of meaner Congressmen,
Directly to his own electorate:
'The United States' immediate defence
Depends upon Great Britain's own success.
Suppose my neighbour's house is burning down.
I help him with my length of garden hose.
What then do I demand? The dollar price?
Or only that he gives it back to me?'
Thus was born the programme of Lend-lease,
By which the British got what they required –
Aircraft by the thousands, tanks and guns,
Small arms and ammunition, sustenance.

'America has become', said Roosevelt,
'The arsenal of world democracy.'

Resolve had brought rewards. Another came –
Though this would later prove ephemeral.
As Winter fell on England, darkening streets
Already dimmed by blackouts and the gloom
That droning bombers brought to city homes,
From far away, from Egypt, news arrived
Of General Wavell's bold initiative.

Now reinforced from England, not content
To wait upon an enemy attack,
He gave O'Connor orders to advance
Across the Western desert, and surprise
The Italian army camped along the coast.
By swift outflanking movements, using tanks,
With armoured cars and mobile infantry,
The British units rapidly progressed
Against a force that far outnumbered them.
Tobruk soon fell, bombarded from the sea,
And down through Cyrenaica they drove
The last remains of Graziani's men;
Until at Beda Fomm, the long pursuit
Was halted by surrender. On the coast
A trail of burning wreckage marked the path
Of Italy's defeat, and into camps
Marched thousands of her soldiers. Fascist dreams
Of empire in North Africa had fled.

Churchill was delighted. 'We have risked',
He told his guests at Chequers, 'sending troops
And vital war equipment from these shores,
Even whilst invasion threatens us,
To give our forces there this very chance
That Wavell has exploited. Now, at last,

This splendid victory has restored our faith
That we can fight aggressively on land.'

The hopes of Mussolini were destroyed,
And Churchill judged the time was apposite
To broadcast to the Italian populace:
'We have for long been friends. Now we're at war.
In Africa your empire lies in shreds
From action by our forces. Why is this?
Italians, I will tell you now the truth.
One man alone has led you to this plight,
This deadly feud with Britain, and the loss
Of long-accustomed sympathy abroad,
Once strong, especially, in the United States.
After unbridled power for eighteen years,
This man has led you now to ruin's verge.
Against the very Crown of Italy,
Against the Pope, the Roman Catholic Church,
Against your wishes, men of Italy,
Who had no lust for war, he has arrayed
The heirs of greatness, old, imperial Rome,
Alongside savage pagans from the north.'

To General Wavell Churchill telegraphed
Congratulations on his victory,
But added that pursuit was paramount:
'Just when the victor is exhausted too,
The vanquished can be forced to pay the most.
Nothing would shake the *Duce* more than this:
A great disaster wreaked in Libya.
No doubt you've thought of harbours to secure
For jumping-off to hunt them down the coast,
Until you meet some real resistance there.
A sickle stroke on people ripe as corn!'

And yet, ironically, Churchill himself
Would stay the sickle at the time most ripe.

And, in his private talk, he made much play
Of how the future history books might claim
He was a criminal gambler, when he'd sent
Such tanks and men to distant Africa,
Who might have turned the scales, if kept at home,
Against invasion of the British Isles.

For one brief morning Churchill could relax.
For with some friends, he went to his old school
On Harrow's windy hill, to which he'd vowed
He never would return. For at the time,
When, as a Liberal, he had strongly backed
The Parliament Bill against the House of Lords,
He had been booed when visiting the school.
Meanwhile, he had admitted gratitude
For how they'd taught him English, and for songs
Which, in his bath, he frequently still sang.

Now, to boisterous cheering, he returned.
He spoke of how the great majority
Of British manhood, now embroiled in war,
Had never had such benefits as those
Enjoyed, right now, by young Harrovians.
So, when this war was over, all must work
To see such privilege more widely shared.

Since Harrow had been bombed, he praised the boys
For sharing in the dangers of this time.
And much to their amusement, Churchill wept,
When they all sang his favourite Harrow songs;
While *Stet Fortuna Domus* was enlarged
By one new verse that praised their famous guest.

That very afternoon he spoke again,
And told the Commons of the desert war:
'This time it's victory for British arms,
For skilful plans and daring officers,

Above all, for the courage of our troops.
Our guarantee to Egypt is made good.
Against all odds, its safety is assured.'
He did not know that Rommel soon would come
To change the face of desert warfare there.

18 Balkan Disasters
Spring 1941

One who knew Churchill well described him thus
At this stage of the war: his health looks good;
His face no longer pale and globular,
But thinner and yet firm. His eyes are strange,
No pouches, no black lines, nor weary lids,
But glaucous, vigilant and combative,
Both visionary and tragic. They're the eyes
Of one who is preoccupied, and loth
To give much need to things of no account;
The eyes of one who faces an ordeal,
Resolved and truculent; perhaps the eyes
Of someone facing great unhappiness.

The Australian Premier also met him then:
'He'll steep himself in gloom about the war,
Bewailing shipping losses, and the threat
Of dire starvation for the populace;
And then proceed to fight his own way out,
Pacing the floor with fury in his eyes,
And uttering some memorable remarks:
"Why do people think this is a time
When years of life are lost, when these indeed
Are years of interest greater than the rest?
Is history past, if we are making it?" '
'He has one tyrant', Menzies later wrote,
'The glittering phrase, that so appeals to him
That awkward facts may fade before its glow.
But this defect comes from his quality.
His course is set. His heart brooks no defeat.'

There was, indeed, more cause for hopefulness.
It was 'a glorious episode', Churchill said,
When speaking to the Commons of the news
That British aircraft, at Taranto Bay,
Had crippled half of Mussolini's fleet,
Including the *Littorio* battleship.
Italian failure, both against the Greeks
And in their own domain of Libya,
Had repercussions no one could foresee.

On one hand stood the Axis Pact of Steel,
And, on the other, Britain's pledge to Greece.
Together these ensured that Balkan war
Would implicate the prime protagonists.
Though angry with his partner, Hitler knew
He could not let the Greeks humiliate
His ally's army in Albania.

As German forces massed towards the east,
Prepared for *Barbarossa* – Hitler's plan
To strike at Russia –some were ordered south,
To rescue Mussolini, and prevent
A British expedition to the Greeks.
For Hitler could recall, as Churchill did,
The Allied armies at Salonika,
Who, in the former war, had played a part
In hastening the Central Powers' defeat.
Would *Barbarossa* also be at risk
From British landings on the coast of Thrace?

On such strategic issues Churchill, too,
Was often musing. How would Turkey act?
How best to use the army of the Nile,
Whose half a million men seemed idle now?
Could British bombers stop the flow of oil
That fed the *Wehrmacht* from Roumania?

Once more these Balkan questions brought to mind
The hopes that foundered at the Dardanelles.

To Eden – now the Minister of War,
In Cairo to review the Middle East –
A telegram was sent to urge support,
If Greece were forced to fight with Germany.
Churchill wrote it from his four-post bed,
Whilst chewing a cigar, and taking sips
Of icy soda water. Someone said,
That when he was composing messages,
Dictating to a staff stenographer,
It was like being present at a birth,
So tense was his expression, so obtuse
The noises he emitted covertly.
And yet there still emerged apt sentences
Of masterly significance and style.

Amidst his many cares, he still found time
To visit Bristol, where he would preside,
As Chancellor, at granting of degrees.
That very night a heavy bombing raid
Struck at the docks, and set ablaze the town.
Next morning, past the ruined homes and fires,
That smouldered on with dull persistency,
An open car conveyed him through the streets.
He waved his hat, and often stopped to meet
The citizens who'd suffered in the raid.
And when he left that evening on the train,
He could not hide his tears at their distress,
And said of them: 'They have such confidence.
I have a grave responsibility.
We must ensure that tonnages of food,
Allotted to such people, are enough
To see them through this great emergency.'

Events were overtaking all the plans
Of British and of Nazi leadership.

Erwin Rommel came to Libya.
And, in Belgrade, a sudden *coup d'etat*
Displaced Prince Paul, who'd favoured Germany,
And formed a government which would now oppose
The passage of the *Wehrmacht* through to Greece.
Hitler, in his fury, took revenge
With unrestricted bombing of Belgrade,
Until the Serbs surrendered. This delay
Would have grave repercussions for his hopes
Of dealing first with Greece, and in the Spring,
Attacking Russia. Winston Churchill urged
A move against the Italians by the Serbs,
But now it was too late. How long could Greece,
Alone against the *Wehrmacht*, still survive?

Briefly another smaller nation State
Diverted his attention, when he met
The President-in-Exile of the Czechs,
Eduard Benes, with a tiny band
Of eager soldiers in their British camp.
They gave him whisky and some special cakes,
And gifts of drawings and embroidery;
Then played their national anthem. As he left,
The sound of *Rule Britannia* bade farewell.

Churchill's advisers, such as Alanbrooke,
Upheld the classic strategy of war,
To concentrate upon one battlefield,
Which, at this moment, lay in Libya,
Where Wavell's army threatened to destroy
The whole Italian expedition force.
Few thought that British help would save the Greeks.

And yet there was a more exalted view.
A promise had been made, before the war,
A British pledge to guarantee the Greeks.
Should Britain break her word? And what effect
Would such dishonour have upon those powers

Whose future actions might be critical –
The Turks especially, and America?

Greece was not a nation to be lost,
Capriciously, abandoned to her fate.
In her lay noble ancestries of art,
The origins of European thought,
And seeds of that democracy, which now
The British Empire struggled to defend.
Such was Churchill's judgment. Nor was he
Devoid of hope that valiant defence
Might stem the tide of Hitler's turpitude.
Why not, upon the ancient soil of Greece,
Where Athens and the bold Miltiades
Had vanquished Persian might, make such a stand?

Eden supported him, and Wavell too,
Despite his chance of desert victory.
Against Italians, Greeks had bravely fought.
With British troops transported there by sea,
And fighter squadrons of the R.A.F.,
The Germans, in the mountainous domain,
Might be frustrated. How might this react
Upon their preparations further north
To strike a treacherous blow towards the east,
Which Churchill now believed were underway?

And so the desert force was much reduced,
When Wavell's soldiers reinforced the Greeks.
They stood upon the Aliakhmon Line,
The British and the Australasians –
Like those at Suvla Bay and Cape Helles,
Who'd faced the Turks beside the Dardanelles –
As German forces concentrated there.

The battle was soon lost. The allied Greeks
Were slow to send their troops from other fronts.

Outflanking movements nullified their hopes
Of holding passes, like Thermopylae.
It was not long before the Greeks themselves
Proposed evacuation. Once again
The British army had no other choice
But fighting to retreat upon the sea.
Memories still were fresh of Dunkirk sands,
Of distant Norway's frozen fjord coast,
And, for the British leader, even now,
The recollection of Gallipoli.

Swiftly a German paratroop descent
Upon the canal at Corinth closed the route
For allied troops still active in the north.
Regardless of air attack, the British fleet
Appeared once more in ports on every coast.
At some, disaster followed. Ships were sunk,
Including several Greek. At Nauplion –
Where Agamemnon may have come from Troy
To meet his fateful end – in that sweet bay,
Were scores of humbler English soldiers drowned.

Churchill became, at this time of defeat,
Most sensitive when anyone discussed
The need for more withdrawals. In one case
A guest at Chequers, General Kennedy,
Had commented that Egypt might be lost.
He was berated soundly for the thought,
And not allowed to mention it again.
There was to be no dwelling on defeat.

Yet even now another threat emerged.
Could British forces hold the isle of Crete?
At Suda Bay they'd built a naval base,
Which gave support to Malta, and sustained
The army based on Suez. Should Crete fall
Then bombers of the *Luftwaffe* might fly

To eastern theatres now in British hands,
And influence the war in Libya.
It was but weakly held. So Churchill urged
Its rapid reinforcement. Freyberg came,
A valiant soldier and a personal friend,
With his division of New Zealanders,
And troops who had survived from mainland Greece.
Their air defence was slight. Yet Churchill knew,
From secret decrypts, of the German plan
To use an elite force of paratroops,
With gliders and a fleet of transport planes.
Invasion ships would also sail from Greece.

The battle was ferocious. Wave on wave
Of airborne soldiers seized the aerodromes,
And fought for their possession hand to hand;
For air control was lacking. British troops,
Entrenched around the runways, watched with dread
As Junker transports ferried in their loads;
And slowly they retreated. Churchill praised
The courage of their leader and his men:
'Your splendid battle's seen by all the world,
And on its outcome, great events unfold.'

At sea the news was different. British ships
Sank many of the *caiques*, which carried troops
From ports in southern Greece. But German planes,
Unchallenged in the air, got swift revenge.
Several vessels fell to *Stuka* bombs.
Briefly, on the island, all was poised.
Lack of armour held the British back,
Although they made repeated, brave assaults.
Soon airborne reinforcements made secure
The German hold on key strategic points,
Especially on the field of Maleme.
At last, from General Freyberg, came the cry
To take survivors off from Cretan shores.

Though subject still to *Luftwaffe* attack,
The navy, yet again, fulfilled its task
Of saving comrades stranded in defeat.

Churchill drew what comfort he could find
In weighing up the cost to Germany.
Their parachute elite, the chosen force
That Herman Goering had especially trained,
Was gravely weakened. Losses were too high
To contemplate a similar event.
Throughout the war, on many diverse fronts,
At no time would the *Wehrmacht* seek to gain
A foothold in the rear of hostile lines
By parachute descent. As Churchill said,
The spear-point of the lance had been destroyed.
Whilst, on the sea, so many men had drowned
From lack of naval shipping in support,
That Hitler and his staff would now abhor
The prospect of invading British soil
Without control of intervening seas.

Yet war in Greece accomplished something more:
The British presence there, alongside those
Whose spirit had informed the western world
For two millennia, had made a mark.
And, generations hence, might be recalled
What British soldiers, lying in repose,
In stony soil amidst the olive groves,
Had given to repay their country's debt.
Their sacrifice had kept her word intact.
A bond was forged, from fire and steel of war,
With past and present, which would long endure
When all defeats and tragedies had gone.

Before the fall of Greece, a crucial step
Was taken by the British Premier.
He sent a note to Stalin, warning him

That Hitler had transferred a powerful force
Of three divisions –panzers – from the south
To southern Poland, near the Russian front.
He naturally concealed the source of this.
The Soviet leader issued no reply.

19 Nadir
Spring 1941

Behind the flurry of these fierce events
In Greece and Crete and in North Africa,
Another scene of war cast sombre shades
On Britain's still beleaguered islanders.
Much of their food and many armaments
Now flowed across the grey Atlantic seas,
Where down below, concealed beneath the waves,
Lay deadly hunters, U-boats of the Reich.

The fall of France enabled them to sail
Far westward from the Bay of Biscay ports
And those upon the coast of Brittany.
In mid-Atlantic lay a band of sea
Unguarded by the Allied air patrols
That flew from mainland bases. In that zone
The U-boat packs could surface and attack.
Their movements were controlled from Germany,
Whence Admiral Doenitz issued his commands
To terrorise the British merchant fleet.
He it was who'd ordered U-boat crews
To rescue no one, since this was a war
For Germany's existence. Thus they fought,
With discipline and courage, for that end.

The losses mounted. British imports fell,
And rationing was tightened. Ships were lost
With vital ammunition, guns and tanks,
With oil and metals, every kind of stuff
That Britain's war economy required.
And merchant seamen perished by the score,
Abiding by the duty war imposed.

How willingly would Churchill have exchanged –
As he himself admitted – an attempt
At full invasion of the British Isles
For this dire peril on the murky sea,
Expressed in cold statistics, charts and curves,
Which threatened strangulation and defeat.

Moreover, in the continental ports,
The surface raiders of the German fleet
Still waited for their chance: in Brittany,
The *Hipper*, *Scharnhorst* and the *Gneisenau*;
And, from German shipyards, stronger yet,
The *Tirpitz* and the *Bismarck* soon would sail.

Bold measures were required. Churchill proclaimed
The battle of the ocean had begun,
As crucial as the battle in the air.
The U-boats must be hunted. Special ships
With catapults to launch a Hurricane,
The strengthening of coastal air command
To guard the sea approach to Liverpool,
The arming of the merchant ships with guns,
Defence of ports along the western coast,
Rapid repairs and fast turn-round of ships,
A greater labour force in British docks:
All these and other steps were introduced.

Churchill meanwhile consulted Roosevelt.
America agreed to further aid
In combating the menace. She'd extend
The area patrolled by US ships,
And build an air base on the Greenland coast.
With Churchill's prompting, Roosevelt offered now
A policy of 'all aid short of war'.
And yet the sinkings rose, and Britain seemed
To feel her life-line ever more constrained.

The British leader, Hitler was informed,
Showed growing signs of weakening from the strain.
Indeed a close confidant said of him
That at this time he was in deepest gloom.
It was what Churchill called his 'black dog' mood,
Which overtook him intermittently.
And yet his resolution was unmoved.
Alanbrooke, the later Chief of Staff,
Who was most sparing in his praise of men,
And critical of much of Churchill's thought,
At this grave time acknowledged his resolve:
'In spite of the vast burden that he bears,
He still maintains a light exterior.
He is the greatest man I've ever met.
From time to time appear such men on earth,
Who stand thus head and shoulders over all.'

In these hard days, when men and women worked
Unceasingly for victory in the war,
It was not Churchill's way to ease their lot,
Except by inspiration in their task.
A label in red capitals might say,
'Action this day', on minutes he had sent.
He hated all excuses and delay.

As for himself, the order of his days
Appeared to others most disorderly.
For half the morning he would work in bed.
At lunch, at which he often drank champagne,
He would discourse in general on the war.
Then, whilst his colleagues worked, he would retire
To have a short siesta. After that
A round of meetings followed, till the time
For dinner – with more drinks – and working guests,
And talk of government matters, and the war.
If at Chequers, or at Ditchley Park,
They'd often see a film – his favourite one

Was Korda's film of Lady Hamilton –
Before, as midnight came, he recommenced
The meetings with advisers: servicemen,
Or politicians, members of his staff,
Who, not much later, would all be required,
Unlike their chief, to reach their office desks.

When he reviewed the war, what Churchill saw
Were losses on all sides and mounting threats.
For most of Europe had by now succumbed
To Hitler's ruthless legions. Any hope
Of forming an alliance in the east
With Balkan States, perhaps with Turkish aid,
Had been destroyed upon the fall of Greece.
When Crete had followed, newer threats emerged:
Of danger to the Alexandrian fleet,
Of more support for Rommel, of attacks
From Cretan airfields on the Middle East –
On Egypt and its vital waterway,
On British-held Iraq, on Syria,
And even on the oilfields of Iran.

Yet in the Commons Churchill still inspired
The deep respect his leadership had earned.
One member said he sounded reasonable,
Authoritative and yet conciliatory.
Nor was his native sense of humour lost.
At one point in a speech he used the phrase
Primus inter pares, which evoked,
From Labour members opposite, the cry
To translate into English. He replied,
'Of course I will', then slowly paused a while,
And, turning to his own backbenchers, said,
'Especially for the old Etonians here!'

At home the scene was dark; for still the blitz –
The night-time bombing of provincial towns –
Brought terror to the British populace.

How long could they withstand the constant loss
Of those they loved, and frightful injuries?
No one could tell. No war before had seen
Such barbarous treatment of civilian lives,
Of women, children, old and sick alike.
Nor could invasion of the British Isles
Yet be discounted. Had not Churchill sent,
Against the wishes of the Home Command,
The bulk of British tanks to Wavell's help?
Who could predict, with certainty, the choice
Of Adolf Hitler, even though it seemed
A *Wehrmacht* strike on Russia was prepared?

Defending on all fronts, what little power
Could Britain summon for aggressive war,
A theme so dear to Churchill ever since
He'd charged the Mahdi ranks at Omdurman?
Her strength alone, however much enhanced,
Could hardly drive the German war machine
Out of those lands at present occupied.
And far beyond the threat of Nazidom
There lay Japan, malignant, keen to prove
Her callous army and her modern fleet
Could master western forces, and create
An Asian empire ruled from Tokyo.

It was no wonder that when Churchill heard
That Britain's largest battleship, the *Hood*,
Was sunk by *Bismarck* with great loss of life,
He showed some symptoms almost of despair.
When, at Chequers, he had heard the news,
He came downstairs to meet his weekend guests.
Hearing the piano played, he shouted out,
'Never play the *Dead March* in my house.'
It was, in fact, a fine sonata piece,
But Churchill would not hear. He cried again,
'I tell you it's the *Dead March*. Stop it now!'

Not all the news was dark. For in Iraq,
Where Rashid Ali tried to gain control
And bind his country to the German cause,
A British column sent from Palestine,
And spirited defence by air force troops,
Expelled him from Baghdad. In Syria, too,
Whose Vichy French connived with Germany
To open airfields to the *Luftwaffe*,
De Gaulle's Free French attacked, with British aid.
A violent battle failed to bring results,
But reinforcements drove the Vichy French
To make an armistice. So Syria,
Where German penetration in the east
Had been a constant threat to Britain's grasp
On Middle Eastern strategy, and oil,
Passed into Allied hands. Then came the news,
Received as Churchill spoke within the House
On how the fall of Crete was imminent,
That *Bismarck*, after long pursuit, was sunk.
'They seemed content', he later wrote of this.

Though Charles de Gaulle's Free French and British troops
Had shared the victory won in Syria,
The friendship of their leaders was in doubt;
For Churchill had declared in Parliament
That Syria would become a sovereign State.
De Gaulle was angered by this disregard
Of French colonial interests. For some time
He'd felt the British were ignoring him.
He publicly condemned their attitude,
Saying they'd connived with Vichy France
To keep its navy out of German hands.

A meeting was arranged at Downing Street.
There were no handshakes. Both became annoyed
At how the staff translated what they'd said.
Interpreters were banished from the room,

Whilst outside, Churchill's secretary feared
A violent confrontation. Who could tell
What depths of fury two such men might plumb,
Unchecked by cautious bureaucrats, like him?
Entrance on a pretext might be wise.
But, summoned by a bell, he was surprised
To find them smoking Churchill's large cigars,
And speaking French in amicable tones.
But soon their angry feelings were assuaged.
They'd recognised their mutual aim in war,
Recalling their initial deep respect
As leaders of their nations. They agreed
On common ways to deal with Syria,
On moderating views that they'd expressed
Of one another's politics and style.

Successful action in the Middle East
Had cost much effort by the Premier.
General Wavell had in his command
No less than five campaigns: in Greece and Crete,
East Africa, Iraq and Syria,
And, in the western desert, where the threat
Of Rommel's intervention cast a doubt
On Britain's whole position. Overstrained,
And struggling even with the further risk
Of Arab-Jewish war in Palestine,
He had at first refused to lend support,
In Iraq first, and then in Syria.

Churchill and the Chiefs of Staff at home,
Insisted on his action. On themselves
They took the full responsibility.
Had either project failed, they would be blamed;
But they agreed that if the Germans reached
Beyond the Gulf of Suez, Britain's chance
Of holding on in Egypt might be lost.
Hitler then would beckon to Japan,

Seize Middle Eastern oil, and from the south
Would menace Russia on a second flank.
So, under orders, Wavell had complied.

But now, in Churchill's mind, a doubt arose
About the General's fitness for command.
He was a valiant soldier, quite prepared
For personal danger, and to bear the brunt
Of constant work with little recompense.
He'd overseen the brilliant feat of arms
That rid the whole of Cyrenaica
Of Mussolini's armies. Victory, too,
Had been his prize in Abyssinia.
Unlike most other generals, he'd agreed
With Churchill's choice to reinforce the Greeks.
Yet was he now the man to face the task
Of meeting Rommel in the desert war,
A general of high initiative,
Who'd played a crucial role in northern France,
And had already cancelled out the gains
That British arms had won in Africa?

Wavell, in fact, was planning an offence
To strike at Rommel unexpectedly,
Before his panzer reinforcements came.
If this bold plan succeeded, well and good.
As Churchill often said, like Bonaparte,
Upon the battle everything would turn.

The House of Commons, unaware of this,
Demanded answers to their earnest doubts
About the grim events of recent weeks.
Why were the Balkans lost? And also Crete?
How serious was the loss of merchant ships,
And fall of imports from America?
What could be done to counter German bombs
That nightly fell on Britain's provinces?

How did the battle fare in Africa
With Britain's army now depleted there?
Was Churchill's government fitted for its task?

When Lloyd George rose to speak, it was soon clear
All this required a vote of confidence.
Aggressively he gazed across the House,
Pointing with his finger constantly.
In gloomy tones, but realistically,
He spoke about the fear of being starved,
About dark chasms, imminent defeat.
'The public must be told the truth', he said.

To hear the man with whom he'd worked so long,
Whose leadership he greatly had revered
In those deep crises of the former war,
Address the House with such foreboding now
Was hard and painful for the Premier.
Was this the man with whom he had campaigned
For radical reform and liberal rights,
By whom he'd sat in Cabinet debates
On crucial issues in the First World War,
Whose eloquence and strength he'd so admired,
Who'd won the war, and managed then the peace?
As Churchill listened to this bitter speech,
He felt, amidst his anger, much regret.
But, after this most critical attack,
Only a great majority of votes
Would now maintain his own authority,
Amongst the public, and in government.

Churchill responded – no one present knew
This was to be the last speech he would make
In that historic Chamber. First he told
Of lobby rumours rife within the House,
Of speculation by the journalists,
Of questions raised in foreign embassies:

How long will this administration last?
Will it break up? Is policy to change?
And yet he welcomed Parliament's debate.
'We still maintain the freedom of this House.
In all the present dangers, this endures.
Of this I'm proud. For this we're fighting now.
In our free country Parliament is free.
How could the government, and its head, myself,
Bear up beneath the burden of this war,
Unless we were sustained by strong support
From this great House and all it represents?'

Standing in his black and crumpled suit,
A huge gold watch-chain on his ample girth,
He had the full attention of the House.
His speech was frank, not that of orators,
As though to kindred, men whom he could trust:
'After our run of desert victories,
The sudden darkening of the scenes of war
Is more especially painful. I confess
I watched the fate of Greece with agony.
But I assure you all we did was done
With full agreement of the Chiefs of Staff,
Though finally decisions are still made
By Ministers responsible to you.
In any case, as Head of Government,
I am the one – when all is said and done –
Whose head should be cut off if we should fail.
I am prepared for this. A far worse fate
Would probably befall – if Hitler won –
The members of this Parliamentary House.
Some people talk as if we could afford
To leave the Middle East, and carry on
To final victory on the sea and air.
Let us not underrate that battlefield.
To lose our hold on Suez and the Nile,
And in the Mediterranean Sea,

Would be a blow we scarcely could sustain.
With all the British Empire's vast resource,
We'll fight for them, and reap a victory.
And though I cannot promise, in the end,
Complete and final victory – yea, I say
That this is my own confident belief:
Victory, at the last, and absolute!
It is a year, within a day or two,
Of that disastrous time, the fall of France.
Men of all parties joined, in that hour,
To fight this business to the bitter end.
We did not know what storms and perils lay
Before us in that year. But nor did Hitler,
When he'd humbled France and saw himself
As Europe's overlord, predict he'd call
On his the German, people to endure
A year of war in nineteen-forty-two.
When I look back upon what's overcome,
On mountain waves through which our ship has
     driven,
When I remember all that has gone wrong,
And what went right, I feel we need not fear
The tempests yet to come. Let them all roar.
We shall come through together, come what may.'

The House divided. There were three against.
It was a triumph for his leadership;
And, as he left the Chamber, cheers burst out,
Spontaneous, from all sides of the House.
Churchill looked pleased. One member said of him:
'Some were a bit defeatist till he spoke.
He cheers them up. Before they were wet-hens,
But now, like bantams, they all strut about.'

That night the House was gutted by a raid.
Its twisted girders framed the open sky,
Like ruined abbeys desolate with time.

Amidst the wreckage, echoes lingered on
Of famous words in British history,
Of which the last defied the German bombs.

'This little Chamber', Churchill once had said,
'Shows how we differ here from Germany.
In virtue of this place, we muddle through
To final victory, and for lack of this
The Germans' sheer efficiency leads them
To ultimate disaster. This small room
Stands as a shrine of this world's liberties.'

20 Operation Barbarossa
Summer 1941

Midsummer came to London. On the Mall
The pale green plane trees stood like sentinels,
Casting their shade on dusty paving stones.
Above Whitehall rose random barrage balloons,
Whose shadows fell, like silent harmless bombs,
Along the fringes of Horse Guards Parade.
The capital city, strangely, was subdued;
Its citizens unruffled, though alert
For sudden air-raid warnings, or the news
Of action overseas, for good or ill.
A few, who briefly strolled within the parks,
Snatching a Summer moment from their desks,
Knew more of what was coming. They had seen
The portents of extraordinary events.

Churchill was intent on *Battleaxe*–
The British plan to thrust the Germans back
Across the western desert, and reverse
The bold advances Rommel had procured.
The Premier had worked with great resolve
To see that Wavell had been reinforced.
He'd overseen dispatch of tanks and guns,
Even at the cost of home defence,
Insisting on the swiftest route by sea.
To Wavell he'd expressed his confidence
That desert victory would bring recompense
For all the battles lost in Greece and Crete.
Tobruk would be relieved, Benghazi freed,
And Egypt and its waterway secured.

Despite the weight that bore on Churchill then,
To some, at least, he still retained his charm.
'He's smaller than I thought, and much less fat',
Said one who met him. 'In his one-piece suit,
Of RAF blue *jaeger*, he is like
A kindly teddy bear. I thought I'd meet
A terrifying, overpowering man.
Instead, he's gracious, with a lovely smile,
And talking to him is not difficult.'

Churchill urged the British to attack
Before new panzer units could arrive
To strengthen Rommel's meagre force of tanks;
But long delays occurred. It would take time –
So Wavell telegraphed – to make repairs,
And train the crews of new, updated tanks.
Moreover, he gave warning of his fears
That British armour was too vulnerable
To anti-tank gunfire and fighter planes.

The Premier was dismayed. Such tardiness,
And seeming lack of spirit of offence,
Had always riled him. What more could he do?
A bomb had nearly killed the Chief of Staff.
'I'm trying', Churchill said, 'to get arranged
A stimulus like that in other spheres.'

At last the action, *Battleaxe*, began.
The British took Capuzzo, near the coast,
But Sollum and Halfaya were still held
By German forces, heavily entrenched.
Then, from the west, the German armour came
And threatened to cut off a Guards Brigade.
Encirclement might follow. Wavell flew
To take control upon the battlefield.
Already there were orders to retreat.
He did no more than to concur with them.

For *Battleaxe* had failed. The British line
Now stood in Egypt where it had begun.
Under orders not to risk too much,
The victor, Rommel, called off his advance,
But once again his leadership had proved
Superior to that confronting him.
By leaving fewer tanks to guard Tobruk,
His flank attack upon the battlefield
Had overwhelmed the British armour there.

Churchill was at home when news arrived
Of General Wavell's failure. All his hopes
Of raising the investment of Tobruk,
Of striking at the heart of Rommel's force
And ending his audacious enterprise,
Had now been dashed. Why hadn't Wavell
Ordered from Tobruk a powerful sortie?

Alone with dismal thoughts, disconsolate,
He roamed the valley in the family grounds.
His doubts concerning Wavell were confirmed.
He knew he was courageous, and had held
A vast command with dignity and skill –
He'd overseen O'Connor's great success
In routing Italian arms in Libya –
But now he was too weary. He had failed
To send sufficient armour into Crete,
And fought with some reluctance in Iraq.
Now *Battlelaxe* had foundered. It was time
To find a new and energetic man.

So Wavell was dismissed with courtesy,
And Auchinleck was summoned in his place.
Churchill had been impressed when Auchinleck,
From his command in India, had sent
The extra troops required to take Iraq.
His leadership had earned him great respect
In earlier commands throughout the war.

So when, at Chartwell, some days afterwards –
Attired in purple dressing-gown and hat –
Churchill had met a member of his staff,
And spoke to him at length of *Battleaxe*,
His main concern was not with the defeat,
But how to take the offensive once again.

Elsewhere, meanwhile, a fateful choice was made;
For Adolf Hitler had at last resolved
To send the mighty *Wehrmacht* to the east
And crush the Soviet Union. This alone
Would end all hope within the British Isles
Of active help in Europe. Goebbels said
That when the Russians fall, the English lose
Their final weapon on the continent.
The air assault had failed; invasion plans
To cross the English Channel had been shelved.
But this one stroke would leave them desolate.

Yet Hitler's motives were, as usual, mixed.
He would pre-empt a possible attack
From Stalin's army. Also, he had feared
The loss of oil, if Russian aircraft bombed
Rumanian fields, so vital to the Reich.
But, most of all, it satisfied his dreams,
Expressed so long before within *Mein Kampf*,
To cleanse the world of Jewish Bolsheviks,
And leave the vast expanse of Russia free
For German exploitation, whilst the Slavs
Became a race of *untermenschen* slaves.

Within his inner circle, Hitler spoke
Of how the Reich would challenge then the world.
Ironically, it would be like the Raj,
The British Empire's rule in India,
Which Hitler much admired for its success
In dominating millions with so few.
As for Russia's military power,

He was contemptuous. Had they not failed
Against the tiny army of the Finns?
And Stalin had destroyed his high command,
In fear of plots against his own regime.

His mind was set. The order was conveyed
To Keitel, Jodl and the general staff
To implement a huge invasion plan,
Codenamed from the medieval king,
The emperor, Barbarossa, who had fought
For unity of Germans, and who slept,
So legend said, until he would return
To recreate a great imperium.

But, under Adolf Hitler, this would be
No Christian war of European knights.
He was explicit. War against the Slavs
Would not be like the battles in the west.
Extermination of all Communists
Was to be ordered by the high command.
Intelligentsia and commissars
Were to be shot or hung without a trial.
Personal scruples must be overcome.
Most sinister of all were special groups
Of SS soldiers, earmarked to destroy
The Jews and gypsies, and the partisans
Who might impede the occupying force.
This was the crude expression of the will
Of Germany's dictator, he who knew
No rule of law, nor Man's humanity.

Churchill was aware of Hitler's plans.
Enigma decrypts kept him well informed.
He could not know for certain that the moves
Of German forces to the eastern front
Were meant for an invasion. But he knew
That Hitler would repudiate his pact
With Marshal Stalin when it suited him,

And that the *Führer*, like Napoleon,
Frustrated by his English enemy,
Might seek to keep his army occupied
By wiping out his one potential foe –
The State of Russia – on the continent.

A personal note from Churchill had been sent
To warn the Russian leader of the threat,
Describing how the *Wehrmacht* had deployed
Divisions freed from Jugoslavia
Along the southern Polish frontier.
The Marshal scorned advice from such a source.

As Ivan Maisky, Stalin's diplomat,
Recalled in memoirs of this tragic time:
'High Summer perfumes filled the earth and air,
Yet signs of thunder filled my heart with dread.
I had already several times informed
Authorities in Moscow of the threat.
I did not wish to believe it. Can it be
That now, tomorrow, any time at all,
The hordes of Hitler will invade our land?'

Soviet forces were quite unprepared
For mass invasion. When the *Wehrmacht* struck,
In three great prongs, they were in disarray.
Along the Baltic coast, towards Smolensk,
And, in the south, to Kiev, swift advance
Entrapped the Russian armies. In the air
The *Luftwaffe* was soon predominant,
Destroying many planes upon the ground.
All seemed to follow *Barbarossa*'s plan
Of cutting off a Soviet retreat
Into the steppelands' vast interior.

Dramatically the course of war had changed.
Again the *Führer*'s one capricious choice
Impelled the fate of nations. What response

Should Britain make to this new chance of war?
To Winston Churchill Russia's Bolsheviks
Had raised a dreadful spectre, which he'd scorned.
A Communist society was 'a plague',
'A bacillus','A foul baboonery'.
He'd argued for a greater allied force
To help the Whites, the anti-Bolsheviks,
And later he was bitterly opposed
To trading with the hated Soviets.
But now his mind, already, was made up.
'If Hitler invaded Hell', he had opined,
'Then I would make a favourable remark
About the Devil to our Parliament.'

A dinner table argument ensued:
On one side, Churchill, with the odd support
Of Stafford Cripps, of left-wing sympathies;
And, on the other, two Conservatives,
Eden and Lord Cecil, both of whom
Were loathe to welcome Stalin as a friend.
Were not the British people still opposed
To any schemes that favoured Communists?
How best to profit from this fateful turn?
Why interfere in self-destructive war,
Waged by dictators full of mutual hate?
These were the only questions of the hour.

But war aroused in Churchill's lively mind
More potent images – of burning towns,
Of innocent peasants slaughtered on their farms,
Of patriots of Russia, bearing arms
Against a new invader of their land.
Now Adolf Hitler was the common foe.
What he embodied in the Nazi State,
That was to be expunged, and all who shared
This worthy aim, whatever was their creed,
Were brothers, nay were comrades, in the cause.

To such a theme his broadcast speech adhered:
'At four o'clock this morning, as you know,
Russia was attacked by Germany.
A non-aggression pact was still in force.
Without declaring war, the Germans crossed
The frontiers of Russia, whilst their planes
Attacked the Russian cities and their troops.
The regime of the Nazis does not lack
The worst excesses of the Soviet State;
But in its cruelty and its love of war,
Efficient and ferocious each in turn,
It far excels all forms of wickedness.
I have opposed consistently for years
The Communism of the Bolsheviks.
I will unsay no word that I have said.
But all this fades away with this new scene
That now unfolds. The crimes and tragedies,
The follies of the past, are nothing now.
I see instead, upon their native land,
The Russian soldiers guarding those same fields
Their fathers tilled from immemorial time.
I see them guarding homes, where women pray –
For there are times when everyone may pray –
I see ten thousand Russian villages,
Where life is wrung so hardly from the soil,
Though children have not ceased to laugh and play.
I see the Nazi war machine advance,
Its arrogant, clanking, Prussian officers,
Its crafty expert agents, and its mass
Of dull, drilled, docile, brutish Huns,
Plodding like a crawling locust swarm.
I see the German aircraft overhead,
Still smarting from defeat in English skies,
Expecting now a safe and easy prey.
My mind goes back across so many years
To when the Russian armies were allied
With us, and France, against the selfsame foe,

And helped to gain a victory, which, alas,
They could not share in. Now I must declare
The policy on which we are resolved,
For we must speak without a day's delay.
How can you doubt what aim we will pursue?
We have one purpose, irrevocable.
We will destroy the Hitlerite regime.
Nothing will turn us from this one pursuit.
We shall not parley, nor negotiate;
But we will fight, by land, by sea and air,
Until the earth is rid of every trace
Of Adolf Hitler, and of Nazidom.
To Russia, and her people, we extend
Whatever help remains within our power.
And to our friends and allies we appeal
To do the same, like us, until the end.
I have a final message to convey:
A deeper motive lies behind this crime.
If Hitler should succeed, he will return
And hurl his forces on the British Isles.
Invading Russia preludes his attempt
To carry out invasion of these isles.
He hopes, no doubt, to beat the Russians down
Before the Winter comes, and turn on us,
Whilst we still stand alone. For long he's thrived
On striking at his victims one by one.
The scene would then be clear for his last act:
The conquest of the western hemisphere.
The threat to Russia is a threat to us,
A threat indeed to the Americas.
Each Russian fighting for his hearth and home,
Fights in the cause of freedom in the world.
Let us redouble all our efforts now,
With strength united, whilst there's life and power.'

Churchill's fear that, if the Russians fell,
Invasion would be swift, was genuine.

153

On hearing grave news from the eastern front,
He sought to bring to greater readiness
The British preparations for defence.
In all ranks of the forces, he declared,
A spirit of attack must be induced.
No building should be lost without a fight.
Each man should have a rifle, or if not,
He should be armed with pistol, mace or pike.
The enemy must struggle for each post
Against intense resistance. Every gain
Must be for him a slow and costly step.
Especially on the airfields, personnel
Must be prepared, as pilots are, to die.
Airgroundsmen should defend the field they serve,
And not rely on soldiers for defence.

The Premier himself quite often shot,
With tommy-gun or rifle, on a range,
To keep himself in practice. None could doubt
That he would sell his life at heavy cost.

To Marshal Stalin, Churchill sent a note
With offers of assistance, and his praise
Of Russian courage and tenacity.
The Marshal thanked him, but was prompt to ask
That Britain should unleash a 'second front',
In Norway, or along the coast of France,
To weaken German efforts in the east.

The Chiefs of Staff, and Winston Churchill, too,
Would not consider such an enterprise.
As Churchill soon replied, the coast of France
Was held by now with German thoroughness.
Mines, pill-boxes, wire and heavy guns
Made landings far too costly. Nor would troops
Be needed by the Germans from the east.
The allied cause would suffer a repulse.

As for raids on Norway or elsewhere,
They could do nothing for the allied cause.
The Russians, Churchill thought, have no idea
How difficult amphibious warfare is.

And yet he promised all aid possible:
Heavy bombing over northern France,
And night raids on the Rhineland and the Ruhr,
To draw from Russian skies the *Luftwaffe*;
Supplies by ship of raw materials;
Hurricane fighters; and in Arctic seas,
Aggressive action by a naval force.
Finally – what was most valuable –
He sent to Stalin information gleaned
From decrypts of *Enigma*: German plans
Relating to their eastern strategy.

21 The Atlantic Charter
Summer 1941

War in Russia eased the present threat
That Hitler might invade the British Isles,
But yet a greater danger would ensue
If Russia were defeated. All the might
Of Germany's armed forces would be free
To turn upon their one remaining foe.
This, indeed, was Hitler's sure intent.
Could Britain then withstand, a second time,
An onslaught from the air, and be prepared
To face invading armies, freshly crowned
With triumph in the east, and new-equipped
For airborne and for maritime descent?
And how long would the precious convoys last,
If U-boat warfare were intensified?

These overwhelming questions taxed the mind
Of Winston Churchill, even though relieved
Of some more urgent worries. Now, it seemed,
The present time was opportune to meet
The one most powerful man not yet embroiled
In open conflict, Franklin Roosevelt;
For he alone could bring his country's strength
To bear upon a European war.
Churchill had foreseen this long before,
Intuitively from his family roots,
And from his long experience and thought
Of how the world had changed since far-off days
Of 'splendid isolation', and the rule
Of half the world by European States.

Some crucial issues had to be discussed.
How could American aid directly help

The Russians in their perilous defence?
Would Britain still receive its vital share
Of U.S. output for its present needs?
Why did American Chiefs of Staff distrust
The strategy of Britain in the war,
Particularly in the Middle East?

What joint approach towards the Japanese
Might temper their aggression? This indeed
Was of the most immediate concern;
For Indo-China had been occupied.
Siam was threatened. Japanese were poised
To strike at Britain in Malaysia,
At U.S. forces in the Philippines,
And at the Dutch in Indonesia.
Roosevelt had made a strong response,
By freezing Japanese assets, and the Dutch
Had cut off from Japan supplies of oil.
In Tokyo these measures would present
A fateful choice of compromise or war.
Without the oil of Indonesia
The forces of Japan could not maintain
Campaigns in China, nor their further plans
For Japanese expansion in the east.

A meeting was arranged. Placentia Bay
Was chosen as an unobtrusive site.
Upon the *Prince of Wales* – a battleship
Which helped to strike the mighty *Bismarck* down –
The Premier embarked, with many aides –
Dill and Pound and Freeman, Lindemann,
Cadogan, Hollis, Jacob and the rest –
For talks would be conducted by the staff,
Alongside those of their political heads.
It was, someone remarked, a retinue
That Cardinal Wolsey would have envied much.

At Scapa, Harry Hopkins then embarked,
Newly returned from Moscow on a quest
To hear directly Marshal Stalin's view
Of how the war proceeded. Weak and tired,
He soon revived in Churchill's company.
A telegram was sent to Roosevelt:
'Harry returned dead-beat, but lively now.
We'll get him in fine trim when we're at sea.
It's twenty-seven years ago today
The Huns began the first of their two wars.
This time we'll make a better job of it.
Twice ought to be enough. With kind regards.'

Atlantic seas were rough. The captain chose
To drop the destroyer escort, and proceed,
Without protection, at a faster speed.
But though the German U-boats roamed the seas,
Enigma now could read their naval code,
So little threat was posed to Churchill's ship.
Yet radio silence had to be observed,
And so, for once, his work was laid aside.

'There was a lull', he said, 'in my routine,
An unfamiliar leisure, not enjoyed
At any moment since the war began.'
He brooded on the future of the war,
The coming battle on the desert sands,
And wrote a memorandum for the staff.
It opened with a salutary remark:
'Renown awaits the general in this war,
Who first restores the art of gunnery
To prime importance on the battlefield,
From which it has been ousted by the tank' –
A prophecy Montgomery would fulfil.

But Churchill now found time for light pursuits.
He read a novel, *Hornblower, R.N.*,

And sent a message to the Middle East
To thank the man who'd recommended it.
'*Hornblower* admirable' was all it said,
But Middle East headquarters were perturbed,
By thinking it a code-word for some plan
Of which their office had not been forewarned.

German spies in Lisbon heard report
That Roosevelt and Churchill soon would meet
Somewhere within the western hemisphere.
When Churchill heard that, as a consequence,
The *Tirpitz* might be sent to intervene,
He curtly said, 'I doubt we'll have such luck!'

On safe arrival, Churchill went aboard
The U.S. ship *Augusta*. There he met
The invalided President, who stood,
Supported by his son, to welcome him.
A choral service for the warship's crews,
And all the highest officers of State,
Was held upon the British quarterdeck.
Draped on the pulpit lay the national flags,
The Union Jack beside the Stars and Stripes.
Churchill chose the hymns. Unwittingly,
'*For Those in Peril on the Sea*' would prove
A poignant choice for many who sang there.
Within four months the *Prince of Wales* was sunk,
Torpedoed from the air in distant seas.

Next day the serious conference began,
With talks on aid to Russia, and the need
For strong defence of North Atlantic routes.
It was agreed to tell the Japanese:
Retreat from Indo-China, and refrain
From all aggressive moves towards Siam.
A powerful warning was included, too,
Drafted by Churchill for the President,

Which gave Japan a notice of intent
To go to war, if she did not desist.

Discussion turned to how they could promote
The principles for which their nations stood,
Especially how the future should unfold,
When peace once more returned. Debate ensued,
For each had national interests to protect.
America was not committed yet
To fight against the Nazis, nor to see
The British Empire strengthen its control
Of African or Asian territories.
Britain, on the other hand, was keen
To make a firm alliance, and ensure
That when the war was over help would come
To keep the world at peace, and prosperous.

Winston Churchill did not disregard
His colleagues in the Cabinet. They were asked
To comment on proposals; so they met,
At two a.m. in London, to discuss
The telegram the Premier had sent.

At last all was agreed. The principles,
Now called *The Atlantic Charter*, were declared:
That neither country seeks aggrandisement,
In territory, or any other way;
That territorial changes should conform
To wishes of the people most concerned;
That people freely choose the form of rule
By which they're governed; and that every State,
Victor or vanquished, all on equal terms,
Should have the right to trade, and be assured
Of access to the world's materials;
That full co-operation in the field
Of labour standards, economic growth
And social welfare should be brought about;

That when the Nazi tyranny had gone,
All men might live absolved from fear and want;
That all, unhindered, might traverse the seas.
And, finally, the belief was reaffirmed,
That every nation would abandon force,
Since future peace can only be maintained
If all who plan aggression were denied
The means to fight by land or sea or air.
And in due time a system might evolve
Which would ensure security for all.

Off the record Roosevelt had said
He would wage war, but not declare it yet.
The attitude of Congress was a bar
To entry into conflict, for, he said,
They would debate the case for many months.
However, he had ordered naval craft
To sink all U-boats threatening British ships.
Churchill was delighted. This would mean
That Adolf Hitler would be forced to choose
Between the risk of transatlantic war
And failure of his submarine campaign.

Yet, overall, the outcome of the talks
Was not as favourable as had been hoped.
The British staff had found their counterparts
Quite unprepared for war. 'It seems remote
From this side of the ocean', one had said.
'The U.S. navy thinks to win the war
Is only not to lose it on the sea.
As for their army, they have no intent
Of fighting for at least a year or two.'

Even Churchill was less sanguine now.
He thought it right to warn the President:
If Russia were compelled to sue for peace,
And hope had died within the British Isles

That U.S. forces would then intervene,
Then none could answer for the consequence.

The powerful warning Churchill had prepared
Against Japan's aggression, threatening war,
Was weakened by the Secretary of State.
The note Japan received gave them no cause
To fear American action. Who could say
What course the Nippon warlords would pursue?

22 Crisis at Moscow
Autumn 1941

The Russians, in their dire predicament,
Demanded aid; not only war supplies,
But now, more urgently, a second front.
Stalin's message was most vehement.
Without a second front, the Russian cause,
Endangered by the *Wehrmacht*'s fresh reserves
Of allied armies and – so Stalin wrote –
Of German troops withdrawn from the west,
Might soon collapse. Within the Ukraine
Factories had been lost; Kiev was taken;
Whilst, at Leningrad, the city faced
A siege throughout the Winter. 'Surely now,'
The Soviet Marshal said, 'a fresh assault
In France, or in the Balkans, can be made
To draw off German troops, and give relief
To Russian armies bearing all the weight
Of war with the invading Nazi hordes.'

Maisky, Stalin's envoy, brought the note,
And later he described how London looked
On that Autumnal ill-foreboding night:
'Bright with moonlight, hastening clouds that shone
With tones of reddish black, that made a scene
Both sinister and gloomy, like a world
Upon the eve of terrible events.'

He met with Churchill, who, in evening dress,
Cigar between his teeth, could only grunt
In bulldog fashion, 'Do you bring good news?'
Sadly Maisky spoke of Russia's plight,
Then asked of Churchill, 'Is this crucial time

A turning point in history? If we lose,
How can you British ever win the war?'
Churchill was sympathetic. He would do
Whatever lay within his power to help,
Including his good offices abroad,
Especially with the U.S. President.

But later, when he wrote to Stafford Cripps,
Ambassador in Moscow with the task
Of putting to the Marshal Britain's case,
He outlined what the Soviets had done
To bring calamity upon themselves:
'The pact with Ribbentrop began it all,
And seizure of the Polish territory.
They looked on while the French were overwhelmed;
That was the second front they clamour for.
Nor were they ready for accord with us
Before the storm of *Barbarossa* broke.
Till then we'd fought alone, while in our midst
The Communists in England did their best
To hamper all our efforts of defence.
If we had lost the battle in the air,
Or been starved out by German submarines,
The Russians would have watched without a qualm.
When Hitler's Balkan escapade began,
Their intervention would have tipped the scales.
They left it all to Hitler. He it was
Who chose at will the moment, and his foes.
That such a government should accuse us now
Of seeking gains in Persia or elsewhere,
Or fighting to the last with Russian troops,
Leaves me quite cold. They distrust our goodwill;
The only cause is self-reproach and guilt.
But do not rub these truths in Russian wounds.
Convince them of our loyalty. Let them know
That we are honest, and have courage too.'

Yet Churchill still insisted on the need
To give what help we could, for as he said,
'If Russia is still fighting, it will help,
And if she stops, our aid will stop as well.'
Beaverbrook and Eden took his part,
But all the Service Ministers and staff
Opposed his plans. Across the table,
Argument was fierce. The R.A.F. –
The critics said – must strengthen air defence,
And should enlarge the British bomber force.
The Middle East, they claimed, was crying out
For fighter planes, like Hurricanes now sent
To fly for Russia on the eastern front.
Army and navy echoed such demands.

Churchill persisted. Every Service Chief
Should make an offer, which must fairly state
What can be spared. At some risk to ourselves,
Both politics and strategy demand
That Russia should be granted some relief.
He looked intently, as he then remarked
That some of his opponents had declared,
When Russia was attacked, she would not last
For longer than three weeks against the Huns.

Debate became acerbic. Churchill scowled.
Most offers were of aircraft out-of-date,
Unwanted guns and tanks or naval craft.
They were rejected. 'Till we can agree,'
The Premier said, 'we will continue here.
We'll stay all night, if that is what's required.'

They stopped for dinner. When they had resumed,
He gave each one a very fine cigar.
'A tribute sent from Cuba', he announced.
'There may be deadly poison in them all.
Perhaps a line of coffins will soon file
Along Westminster Abbey's ancient nave.'

In half an hour the long debate had closed,
And aid for Russia was at last assured.
Churchill had made a final wise remark,
Echoing what Roosevelt had said,
'America, not us, will have to be
The major arsenal of the Soviets.'

Meanwhile the Russians undertook to share
Control of Persia with a British force.
Britain had hoped that Persia would agree
To rid itself of German influence,
But oil was threatened, and the central route
For aid to Russia through the Persian Gulf.
After a brief campaign by British troops,
The Shah surrendered, and from north and south
The two invading powers then took command.
As Winston Churchill said, with some regret,
'The laws are silent in the midst of war.'

In Britain now there was a kind of pause.
While greater conflicts thundered on abroad:
On Russian steppes, along the Baltic shores,
In Africa, and far away at sea.
People grumbled, but made few complaints.
German bombers came less frequently,
And not so many shattered homes were seen.
Churchill was still immensely popular.
He went to visit aircraft factories,
Where Communism flourished, but at these
The workers gave vociferous applause –
Though it was said that output had not grown,
Until the Soviet Union was attacked.

But at this time the Premier was apt
To get frustrated at the seeming lapse
Of British action on the scene of war.
To Auchinleck he bitterly complained

For his delay in launching an attack.
The general came to London to present
The reasons for his caution. Churchill hoped
That face to face discussion would make clear
The need to act much sooner than was planned.

General Ismay briefed the visitor
On Churchill's strengths and foibles. He explained
That normal standards could not be applied.
'He is a leader high above the rest.
None can replace him. Sometimes he will be
Respectful of tradition, dignified;
But, when the spirit moves him, he becomes
A gamin, whom convention cannot rule.
Enthusiasm, courage, industry
In him are boundless. He is always loyal.
A soldier who'd engaged the enemy
Need never fear the loss of his support.'

The Chiefs of Staff and Churchill were impressed
By Auchinleck's persona and command.
'He is the best man, even if he's wrong',
Was Churchill's wry conclusion. He preferred
This general, who was argumentative,
To one, like Wavell, who was taciturn
And fond of poetry, even in the war.
Auchinleck was determined. None could shake
His soldierly decision to prepare
The next offensive in his own good time.
In vain did Churchill argue that delay
Might favour Rommel, too, with extra tanks.

On Churchill's orders more divisions went –
Against advice from cautious Ministers –
To strengthen further Auchinleck's offence.
He argued also for a naval force
To hunt Italian ships that carried oil

And other vital cargoes for the use
Of Axis armies in the desert war.
Increasingly he saw the next campaign –
Codenamed *Crusader* – as the crucial step
In Britain's re-emergence in the war.

He thought of how the British would advance
To take the whole of Cyrenaica,
And then drive out the Axis totally.
Invasion then could move to Sicily;
A second front in Europe would be won.
The Vichy French in Tunis might be swayed
To turn upon their German overseers.
Perhaps, indeed, with Roosevelt's support.
Turkey, also, might be influenced,
By British victory in North Africa,
To be, at last, a new belligerent,
And bar the way through Anatolia.
Even in Norway Churchill saw a hope
Of aiding Russia by a landing there,
And winning Sweden to the allied cause.
To Roosevelt he sent ambitious plans.
Massive armoured forces could be used,
Within two years, to land on Europe's shores,
And give support to nationalist revolts
Against the hated Hitlerite regimes.
All this would follow desert victory.

Experts, like Alanbrooke, were not impressed.
He'd learnt the lesson of the harsh defeat
Of British troops in Scandanavia.
Forced to defend his views at Downing Street,
He found the Premier in angry mood.
Details were questioned. 'Why so slow to move
Along the road from Trondheim?' Churchill asked.
'Enemy resistance, clearing blocks,
Repairing damaged bridges', Brooke replied.

For two hours he was tested on his plans,
Facing remarks whose bitterness was due
To Churchill's disappointment at the lack
Of readiness to fight aggressively.
Alanbrooke would write that such ordeals
Were excellent training for his later task
As Chief of the Imperial General Staff,
When often he would challenge Churchill's plans,
And face the wrath at his temerity.

Others denied that Sicily was ripe
For any action in the time foreseen;
Nor did they think the Turks would yet advance
Beyond their present dull neutrality.
Moreover, they now emphasised the threat
To Britain's eastern Empire from Japan.
Were we neglecting Singapore's defence,
Rangoon and Burma, even India?

The Chiefs of Staff proposed a modest plan:
Defence of Egypt and its waterway,
Of Basra and the southern Russian flank.
If Auchinleck succeeded, their advice
Was soldier on to Tripoli, and get,
With French connivance, North-west Africa.

Churchill was depressed by such a lack
Of broad ambition and offensive drive,
But, once again, he would not overrule
The judgment of the Chiefs, if they agreed.
Referring to *Crusader*, he proposed
To take no view of what the future held
Until he knew the outcome; for, he said,
A battle is a veil. It is not wise
To try to peer through such obscurity.
Yet, to his son, he vented his dismay:
'The Admirals, Generals and Air Marshals chant

Their stately hymn of always "Safety First",
Whilst Shinwell and the other critics blame
My government for its failure to advance.
Amidst all this I have to be restrained
By sitting on my own pugnacious head!'

There is no doubt that Churchill was beset
By many problems, not the least of which
Was how to share the limited supply
Of war equipment and of fighting men
Amongst the many claimants – Home Command,
The army, air force, navy overseas,
The Russians and imperial defence.
'I am', he said, 'a keeper in a zoo,
Distributing half-rations to the beasts.
But yet', he added, 'luckily they know
I am an ancient keeper, and their friend.'

Beneath his wit and camaraderie,
One deep concern lay ever in his mind.
If Russia were defeated, he well knew
That all the might of Hitler's war machine
Would soon be turned on Britain. German strength,
Enhanced by victory, would be sure to grow,
As Europe's subject nations, quite prostrate,
Supplied the *Herrenvolk* with all the means
Of unrestricted warfare – food and steel,
New armaments and labour. Surely then
The power of Britain, howsoever built
On moral worth and steadfastness of will,
Could not sustain a brutal new assault,
Or keep the sea-lanes open to the west
Against a vast updated U-boat fleet?

The only hope would be America.
Soon, indeed, the President would get
A Bill through Congress, giving him the right

To arm his merchant ships against attack.
But yet how far the New World was from war!
What had the British Staff reports observed?
The American army had no taste for it,
And even sailors had no thought beyond
Protection of the convoys. For the rest,
In Congress and amongst the populace,
The war was distant European news,
Not touching them, except in sympathy.

Uncertainty prevailed on every front.
Churchill recalled a saying which described
The life of man as like a single walk
Along a passage closed on either side.
As windows are approached, an unknown hand
Opens each one; and yet the ensuing light
But heightens still the darkness at the end.

These thoughts did not deter the Premier
From sounding full of hope, when he addressed
The Lord Mayor and his guests at Mansion House.
'The future and its mysteries', he opined,
'Remain to us inscrutable, and yet,
What's plain to me is that the blood-stained hands
Of Nazis and their quislings will not rule
The famous States of Europe for too long.
Their cruelty has engendered in their hearts
A consciousness of insecurity.
They, not us, will live with growing fear.'
Despite his personal doubts, still Churchill said
That we may find America at war.
'And now, meanwhile, we greatly benefit
From their most generous aid. The Lend Lease Bill,
Which proves that money does not rule the hearts
Of people in the great democracy,
Must surely be the most unsordid act
Of any nation in recorded time.'

How valid was the widely held concern
That Russia might collapse? Was victory near
For Hitler's huge invasion? Would he prove
That, even where Napoleon had failed,
He could subdue the Russian wilderness?

Indecision in the high command
Had slowed the *Wehrmacht*'s progress earlier.
Hitler had overruled his generals' plans
To march on Moscow, for he still preferred
To capture first the basin of the Don,
And then advance to Baku's oil supplies.
But now, as Autumn came, he gave the word
For Moscow to be taken. Great success
Soon followed at Vyazma. Russian troops,
Near half a million, were encircled there.

In Berlin, Goebbels readily announced
That Timoshenko's group had been destroyed,
And this had brought the conflict to a close.
Then, not long after, German armour stood
Prepared to drive on Moscow – once again
With pincer movements from the north and south,
As they had done at Kiev and Bryansk.

Soon they would reach the suburbs. Fear had struck
The people and authorities within.
So Stalin's secret police were drafted in
To maintain order. He himself was prone
To lose control in times of deep despair.
Was he recalling how, at Brest-Litovsk,
His predecessor, Lenin, had contrived
To grant immense concessions of the land
To make peace with the Kaiser's Germany?
Would promises to distant Britain count
Against this desperate circumstance of war?

Meanwhile, Hitler, sure of Moscow's fall,
Anticipating but a ruined site,
Was not deterred by warnings. He replied,
'What cannot be achieved in Winter now,
We'll carry out next Summer.' Then he planned
A campaign further east, with bolder aims –
To gain possession of the Russian soil,
Turn the Crimea into German land,
A *Gau* within the Reich, a settlement
For purest ethnic types, once purged of Slavs.
With Goebbels he discussed the colonies
That Germany would build and then exploit.
His dreams had not abated, even though
His Minister, Fritz Todt, expressed the view
That arms alone would not conclude the war;
That it could only end by politics.

Churchill and his chief advisers knew
How there, near Moscow, hung the fate of all.
If Russia fell, the whole assembled power
Of Germany could turn, at Hitler's will,
Upon the British Isles. A trifling act,
Played out within the House of Commons, showed
How tense the pressure bore upon him now.
Questions, critical in tone, had come
From Waldron Smithers, Conservative M.P.,
About the office held by Lindemann.
What was he paid? Was he an alien?
Churchill was livid. How could they attack
His faithful friend and expert counsellor,
Who on so many vital matters gave
Such scientific, prompt and shrewd advice?
Afterwards, when Waldron Smithers came
To meet him in the Smoke Room of the House,
He shouted to the shocked M.P. to leave:
'Just get the blazes out of here!' he roared,
'I never want to speak to you again.'

173

Who, at this moment, could foresee the days,
Not long in coming, when the Winter snow,
The bitter Russian winds and freezing earth,
Would paralyse both soldiers and their arms;
When men would die from frostbite, engines stall,
And German generals read, beside their maps,
The dreadful words of Caulaincourt's account
Of how Napoleon's army met its fate?
Who knew that Zhukov, newly in command,
Would launch a fresh offensive, which would strike
The German army when most vulnerable?
And who could know that his most valued troops
Were fresh reserves from far Siberia,
Released by news that Japanese intent
No longer threatened Russian territory?

No prophecy of such a turning point
Was entertained in London at this time.
The news was grim. The Russians were besieged.
How could they long evade the final blow
Of Hitler's deadly *Wehrmacht*? Only faith,
Alive within the breasts of Englishmen,
Especially in their leader, gave them hope
In some unknown stroke of Providence.

23 The Failure of Crusader
Autumn 1941

All Churchill's hopes were pinned on Auchinleck.
His victory was the key that would unlock
The door to Britain's progress in the war.
Early in November, at full moon,
He would attack the desert enemy.
His plan, endorsed by Churchill, was to smash
The armour first, in Cyrenaica,
Relieve Tobruk, and drive the Axis back,
If all went well, as far as Tripoli.

Once more the general asked for a delay.
Two weeks, he said, were needed to perfect
His long-prepared offensive. This request
Infuriated Churchill, who'd prepared
A secret note to Franklin Roosevelt,
Informing him when battle would commence.
'How can I say to Parliament', he said,
'And to the nation, how our armies stand
Without engagement for so many months,
Whilst Russia bleeds to death from day to day?'

Yet Churchill had no choice but to concede.
He recognised he could not force the hand
Of generals who commanded far away
And saw precisely what was needed there.
In fact, the new delay proved favourable,
Since in that time the British navy sank
A large proportion of the merchant ships
That carried fresh supplies for Rommel's force.

The Premier sent a message from the King
To all ranks under Auchinleck's command,

Which emphasised His Majesty's belief
That all would be devoted to their task.
And Churchill added his own clarion call:
'This battle will affect the future course
Of this whole war. The hardest blow yet struck
For victory, home and freedom is to hand.
Your desert army may contribute now
A page in Britain's finest history,
To rank with Blenheim and with Waterloo.
The eyes of every nation look on you.
Our hearts are with you. God uphold the right!'

At last, *Crusader* started – none too soon,
For Rommel was preparing an attack
Upon the British stronghold at Tobruk
That lay behind his lines. Unbalanced now,
The Axis forces gave way to the north,
And lost their hold upon the vital ridge
Of Sidi Rezegh. But it was not long
Before the *Wehrmacht* tanks, held on the coast,
Arrived in force to drive the British back.
An armoured melee followed. Churchill sent
Enigma decrypts, telling Auchinleck
Of Rommel's fears of shortages of fuel.
But German tactics were superior,
For, as before, they led the British tanks
Into the sights of anti-aircraft guns.
Totensonntag, Germans called this day,
For their own losses were substantial too,
But Axis' tanks secured the battlefield,
With Sidi Rezegh in their hands again.

Stirred by victory, Rommel made a raid,
Of characteristic boldness, to the east.
He crossed the Egyptian frontier, spreading fear
And causing much confusion in his wake.
Cunningham, the general in command,

Considered a withdrawal. Loss of tanks
Inhibited his spirit of offence.
In this grave crisis, Auchinleck held firm.
The general was dismissed, and in his place
The Chief of Staff from Cairo took command,
With orders to continue the offence.

From London, Churchill heartily endorsed
The brave decision Auchinleck had made.
'And since you've saved the battle', he went on,
Why not proceed to win it? Take command!
Your presence at the front inspires them all.'
But Auchinleck reluctantly declined:
'From GHQ at Cairo', he replied,
'The whole course of the battle can be seen.'
He would not yield to Churchill's further pleas.

Wireless breakdown and a lack of fuel
Impeded Rommel's daring enterprise,
Whilst, at Tobruk, the British garrison
Had staged a break-out, threatening now to meet
Advancing columns of *Crusader*'s force.
The panzer leader hastily returned.
His presence re-ignited Axis' hopes.
Although Tobruk could no more be contained,
The British armour suffered heavy loss
At El Haseiat. Yet Auchinleck had won,
For Rommel's total casualties were high,
And he withdrew to the Gazala line.

This was a victory, but inadequate.
There was to be no move on Tripoli.
The Axis force was weakened but intact,
And Churchill's plans to stimulate the French,
And gain control of North-west Africa,
Had come to nought. He'd also been proved wrong
In his advice – though others had concurred –

For he had welcomed Auchinleck's intent
To concentrate against the Axis' tanks.
'The principle is right', so Churchill wrote.
He'd quoted Bonaparte: '*Frappez la masse ....*'
But he, and his commander, had ignored
How flexible the armour had become,
Especially under Rommel, who had seen
That armour could be lured to desert traps,
To vital points upon the battlefield,
Where it was then destroyed defending them.

This stalemate in the desert shattered hopes
Of future progress Churchill long had held.
Where could he turn for any evidence
That Britain could reverse the tide of war?
A shrewd observer saw him at this time
As looking very fresh and young and spry.
'He seems quite cheerful, truculent perhaps,
But underneath there is more caution now.
Vigour and purpose in his public face
Belie the fact that he will hesitate
Confronted with severity of risk.'
And then he added – with some relevance –
'He would not be found wanting, that is sure,
If he were fighting in the final ditch.'

That moment had not come; yet even now
The state of conflict was most critical.
All eyes were turned on Moscow. There, perhaps,
The history of the war might run its course.
If German soldiers, frozen and fatigued,
Could summon up a last reserve of strength,
And break the will of Stalin to resist;
If Russians, like their fathers, now declined
To die to save the Motherland from death,
The war might be resolved Who then could stand
Against the will of Hitler? None could see

That, in the outcome, other forces too,
Both godly and demoniac, would prove
As powerful as this clash of tyrannies.

24 Pearl Harbor
Winter 1941

Winter had come to England, cold and grey,
A pale reminder of the Moscow scene,
Which reinforced the sense of dogged gloom
Of people now immured to life at war.
There was small cause for hope. Yet few would speak
Of seeking terms with Hitler. None foresaw
That now, across the globe, one stark event,
One swift and violent action, like a flame
That flares up from an unseen burning glass
And soon becomes a spreading forest fire,
Would shift the present boundaries of war,
Till all the world was charred with the effect.

Above the hills of northern Oahu
The planes of Admiral Yamamoto's fleet
Flew low towards Pearl Harbor. They had come,
Through seas obscured by fog, from Kurile Isles,
Unseen by any foreign ship or plane,
And now flew freely, like a host of birds
Released from cages, seeking out their prey.
Tightly in harbour lay the massive ships
That seemingly had ruled the vast expanse
Of peaceful ocean. Now the word was sent,
And 'Tora, Tora, Tora', went the cry.
Surprise had been achieved. Pearl Harbor lay
Inert and still; of war incredulous.

Dive-bombers first, and fighters, wheeled aside
To blast the fields where aircraft stood in ranks,
Some primed with petrol, ready to explode
When bomb or bullet struck. Then came the turn

Of low torpedo planes that skimmed the docks.
From helpless warships flames and smoke sprang up.
The billowing clouds, of flickering red and black,
Cast darkness on the havoc of the decks,
And deep in hulls the gaping holes betrayed
Both crews and vessels to the greedy sea.

With one great blow the Japanese had gained
Control of the Pacific. Now the lands
Of south-east Asia – Burma and Siam,
The Dutch East Indies, and the Philippines,
Pacific islands, some American,
And even Australasia – had come
Within the range of their offensive power.
Invasion fleets already were at sea,
Moving southwards, threatening to extend
Their martial force beyond the China Sea.
In Indo-China airfields were prepared
For bombers to assist the land campaigns.
Colonial powers, the British and the Dutch,
The U.S.A. within the Philippines,
And all of eastern Asia were besieged
By atavistic warlords of Japan.

Churchill had said, so many years before,
'I don't believe there is the slightest chance
That, in our lifetime, we shall fight Japan.'
Now he was at Chequers, dining there
With Harriman and Winant. He seemed tired,
And sat immersed in thoughts. From time to time
He even held his head between his hands.
The wireless was turned on to hear the news
About the Russian front and Libya.
A few brief words were added at the end
Of some attack on shipping at Hawaii.
It did not sound important at the time.

But then the butler came into the room.
'It's true', he said, 'We heard it all outside.
The Japanese attacked Americans.'
The three men at the table looked askance.
Then Churchill rose, and made towards the door.
'War on Japan will be declared at once.'
'Good God!' said Winant, 'How can you do that?
You've only heard it on the radio!'
Churchill stopped, and looked half-quizzically.
'What shall I do?' He only sought advice
About the proper diplomatic steps.
'Let me phone first', the Ambassador replied.

Churchill waited. Then he also spoke:
'What's this about Japan?' 'It is quite true.
They have attacked Pearl Harbor.' Then a pause.
'We're in the same boat now', said Roosevelt.
'Tomorrow I will ask our Congress here
To openly declare hostility.'
'Our declaration', Churchill then replied,
'Will follow yours, within at most an hour.'

Without delay the Premier arranged
The summoning of Britain's Parliament,
And told the Foreign Office to prepare
A declaration of the state of war
Between the United Kingdom and Japan.
To Chiang Kai-shek a telegraph was sent:
'The British Empire and the U.S.A.
Have always been your friends, but now with you
We face, as one, a common enemy.'

For many months the danger from Japan
Had troubled Churchill and his government.
At first he had agreed with Chiefs of Staff
That, after Britain, not the Middle East,
But Singapore, should have priority

In matters of imperial defence.
Yet later, as the desert war advanced,
And he'd envisaged victory in that sphere,
He'd reneged on this plan. Egypt's defence
Would only be abandoned for the need
To save the lands of Australasia.
He knew it was a calculated risk.
Like others, he believed the Japanese
Would not embark on new aggressive moves
Whilst still embroiled in China. He well knew
They feared the Russian army in the north,
And surely would not contemplate a war
Against the united navies of the west.
Yet when they took control, from Vichy France,
Of Indo-China, tension had increased.
For Roosevelt, supported by the Dutch,
Imposed an oil embargo on Japan.
The choice was stark: to fight or to withdraw.
And then the warlike Tojo came to power.

Above all else, what Churchill then had feared
Was war against the European States
That did not thus directly interfere
With any interests of America.
Whatever Franklin Roosevelt might feel,
The U.S. Congress might not go to war
To save the British Empire, or the Dutch.
If this should happen, Britain was too weak
To save Malaya; even as the Dutch
Could not alone defend their territories.

Notwithstanding, Churchill made it clear
That if Japan attacked a British State
Then war would follow. To this end he'd sent
A naval squadron out to Singapore,
Despite the protests of the Admiralty,
Who did not want to weaken their defence

Of convoys in the western hemisphere.
On Churchill's orders *Prince of Wales* had gone,
The newest first-class battleship afloat.
None could foresee how soon it would be sunk,
A few days after war had been declared.

The shock of what the Japanese had done
Awoke in Churchill hopes he'd long concealed.
Despite Pearl Harbor's tragic pain and loss,
It was to him the greatest joy to know
America would fight at Britain's side.

'I could not then predict the course of war.
Nor had I seen how mighty was Japan,
But I was sure we'd won', he later wrote.
'After Dunkirk, and then the fall of France,
The agony we went through at Oran,
The invasion threat when we were scarcely armed,
The blitz upon civilians in our towns,
The deadly struggle of the U-boat war,
After our fighting all alone so long,
After my duty under so much stress,
At last I knew that we would win the war.
Britain would live, the British Empire too,
The Commonwealth of Nations would endure.
How long the war would last, how it would end,
No man could tell, nor did I even care.
For once again our nation would emerge,
However mauled, still safe, victorious.
We should not be destroyed. As for our foes –
The fate of Adolf Hitler was now sealed,
And Mussolini's. What then of Japan?
They would be ground to powder. All the rest
Was but the use of overwhelming force.
Britain, Russia and the United States,
Unified in very life and strength,
Were twice or thrice the power of those opposed.

Doubtless it would take time. Much would be lost,
Especially in the east. Yet all would pass.
Disaster, tribulation would ensue,
But, in the end, it would all come aright.
Some might discount American intent,
Their willingness to fight, their hardiness,
Their unity and democratic style,
But I', so Churchill wrote, 'had studied how
They'd fought their civil war so desperately.
American blood was mingled in my veins.
Tired from emotion, thanking Providence,
I slept that night as one who had been saved.'

'The end of the beginning', Churchill said.
A massive task still lay ahead of him,
But Britain had not lost, that much was sure.
The burden of the conflict, all alone
Against the might of Hitler's Germany,
Was lifted from the British islanders;
And from their leader, whose brave shoulders bore
So many shocks of battles lost in France,
In Norway, Greece and Crete, and on the seas.
His courage had not failed. He was, indeed,
The saviour of his country; one who'd plucked
The flower of safety from the sting of death.

Principal Sources

Addison, P., Winston Churchill, OUP, 2007.

Churchill, W.S., *The Second World War*, Vols 1-3, Cassell, 1948-50.

Churchill, W.S. (ed), (grandson), *Never Give In*, Pimlico, 2003.

Colville, J., *The Fringes of Power*, Vol 1, Sceptre, 1986.

Duchesne, J. (alias for Michel Saint-Denis), *Deux Jours avec Churchill*, Editions de l'Aube, 2008.

Gardiner, J., *Wartime Britain 1939-1945*, review, 2005.

Gilbert, M., *Finest Hour*, Heinemann, 1983.

Jenkins, J., *Churchill*, Pan Books, 2001.

Kershaw, I., *Hitler 1936-1945*, Penguin, 2000.

Liddell Hart, B., *History of the Second World War*, Pan Books, 1973.

Nicolson, H., *Diaries and Letters 1939-1945*, Collins, 1967.

Soames, M., *Clementine Churchill*, Cassell, 1979.